*Yesterday's Connecticut*

## Seemann's Historic States Series

No. 1: *Yesterday's Florida* by Nixon Smiley
No. 2: *Yesterday's New Hampshire* by Richard F. Leavitt
No. 3: *Yesterday's California* by Russ Leadabrand, Shelly Lowenkopf & Bryce Patterson
No. 4: *Yesterday's Indiana* by Byron L. Troyer
No. 5: *Yesterday's Michigan* by Frank Angelo
No. 6: *Yesterday's Connecticut* by Malcolm L. Johnson

# Contents

*Acknowledgements* / 7
Introduction / 9
Growing with a New Nation / 29
New Citizens, New Cities / 53
The Modern Era—Less Steady Habits / 119
*Index* / 143

# *Acknowledgments*

FOR VARIOUS REASONS, old photographs are not always easy to come by, and this book could not have been assembled in anything like its present form without the cooperation of John F. Beegan, *Hartford Courant* news librarian, and his staff. Many of the photographs reproduced in this book were assembled during the 200th anniversary of *The Courant,* and my thanks are also due to Charles L. Towne, editor of the editorial page and associate editor, and to James J. Devaney, now of the Society for Savings, for providing a huge source of old photographs from which to choose. The contributions of *The Courant* can be seen in the number of photographs labelled HC. Also of great help was David N. Palmquist of the Bridgeport Public Library, whose contributions are indicated with BPL. A number of New Haven area pictures were obtained from the New Haven Redevelopment Agency and are labeled NHR. Private individuals who contributed included Marcantonio Squatrito of Manchester, John Massaro of Milford, Francis Newell of Glastonbury, Doris Barton of North Haven, Frances Cooper Doolittle of Hamden, Florence Young of Milford, and Jean Gamsby Liefeld of Hamden.

The single most important source for research for the text and captions was the official history of the state, Alfred E. Van Dusen's *Connecticut,* published by Random House. Another *Connecticut,* compiled by the Connecticut Writers Project during the Depression, was also helpful, as were *The Indians in Connecticut* by Chandler Whipple (the Berkshire Travelers Press), and a number of Connecticut Tercentenary publications. Again, the files of *The Hartford Courant* were invaluable, as were the reference works at the Connecticut Historical Society and the Connecticut State Library.

Certainly the most important contribution to this book came from members of my family, however. My wife, Betty Jean Carper Johnson, researched captions, found old photographs and post cards, made telephone calls to historical societies and archives, and generally displayed remarkable patience with the absences of the author. My parents, Ernest W. and Marjorie Leishman Johnson, acquired photographs from their friends and relatives, and my brothers, Roderick C. Johnson and Richard Johnson, were both helpful in finding pictures and information about the New Haven area.

*Hartford, 1976*                                                                          Malcolm L. Johnson

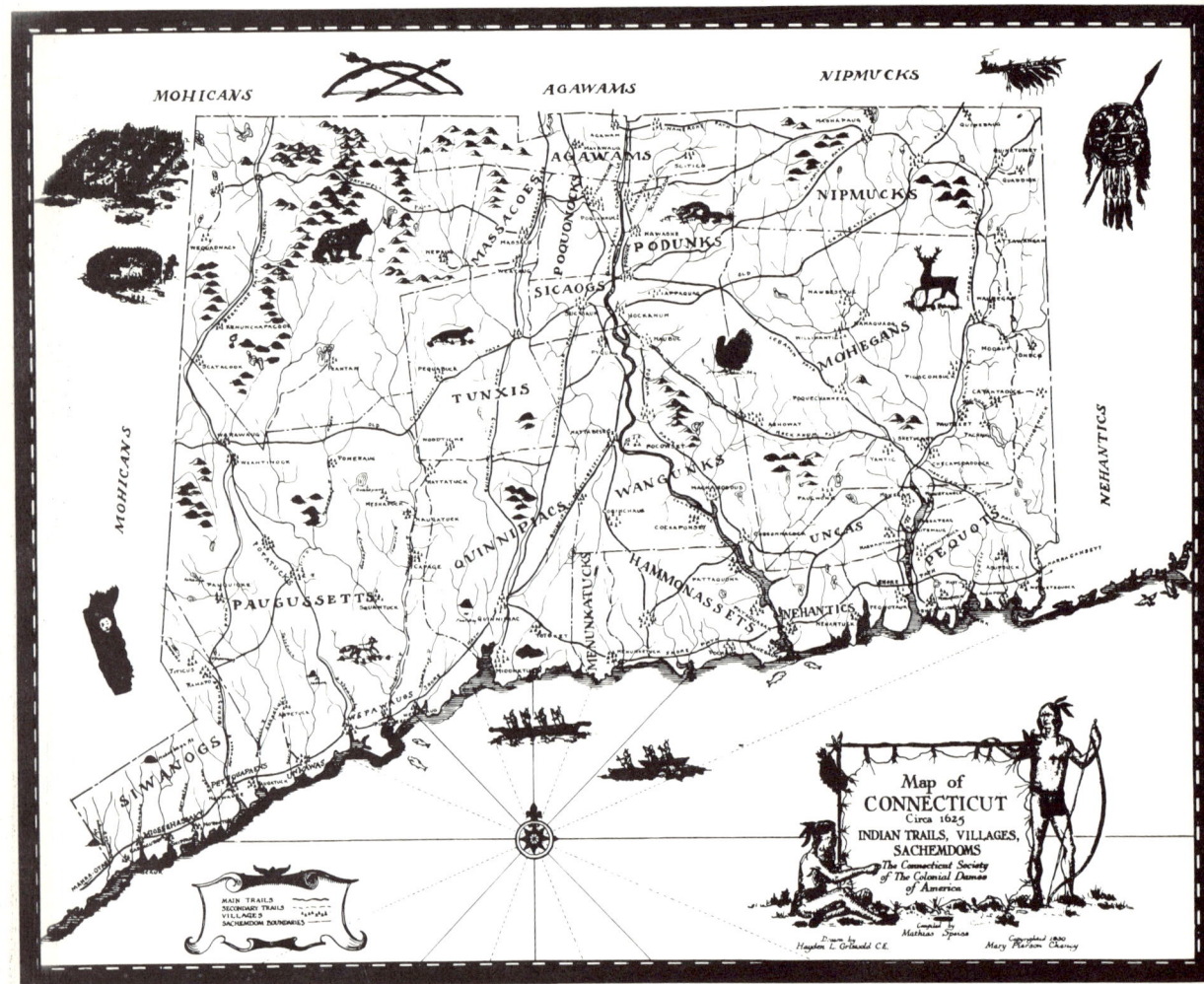

THIS MAP shows how Connecticut's Indians divided up the state in 1625, five years after the Pilgrims landed. The map was compiled in 1930 for the Connecticut Society of Colonial Dames.

# *Introduction*

CONNECTICUT is often thought of as the "country," perhaps because that is what it was to sophisticated New Yorkers who fled the city in movies and plays of the thirties, forties, and fifties. The image persists, even today, because to a Manhattan-based writer or executive, the "country estates" or "farms" or wooded retreats of the western part of the state provide at least an illusion of rusticity. But a ride up Interstate 95, which cuts through the southern part of the state from Greenwich to Stonington, provides, especially on its western end, a forcible disclaimer to visions of white clapboard hamlets and green woodland. Here one sees urban sprawl at its greyest. There is pollution in the air (the worst in the country in 1975—except for Los Angeles, of course) and the harbors along Long Island Sound are surrounded by industrial ugliness: fuel storage tanks, and huge power companies filling the sky with wires and smoke. Rundown cities have skylines dominated by towers of glass, plastic, and manufactured stone. This certainly is not "the country," nor is it "old New England."

Off the beaten track, of course, one can find a more beautiful Connecticut in the small towns in western Connecticut, in sections of a large city like New Haven, or a smaller one like Norwich. And throughout the state, especially in the Litchfield Hills and lower Connecticut River valley, stretches of the state's pristine natural beauty remain, almost unspoiled by more than three centuries of progress and growth.

A great deal has been lost, however, most of it in the past half century. And architectural conservancies are just beginning to move to arrest the destruction of the older parts of the cities of Hartford and New Haven, historically the most important cities in the state. The existence of Yale University as a presence and an influence has retained a good deal of old New Haven in any case; a good part of the downtown area of the city looks today almost as it did a century ago. Hartford has lost much more, and it is uncertain even now how much of the nineteenth-century city can be preserved. Only recently, the old turretted, Richardson-esque YMCA building, which faced Bushnell Park and complemented the post-Civil War Memorial Arch, was destroyed—despite the efforts of the Hartford Architecture Conservancy to save it. Also razed recently was the turn-of-the-century Garde Hotel with elegantly detailed brickwork that bordered the park.

Because Hartford is the capital city and because so much of its past has been destroyed, an attempt has been made in this book to recapture a sense of what the city was like in the years between the Civil War and the modern era that began with the twenties. But more than this, *Yesterday's Connecticut* attempts to present glimpses of important aspects of Connecticut's past throughout the state, and of its people: manufacturers, merchants, show people, and the people who ran its small businesses on its Main Streets of yesteryear.

*February 1976*                                                                                              Malcolm L. Johnson

NEW HAVEN'S GOVERNOR Theophilus Eaton built his mansion in the shape of the letter "E." and it is said to have had twenty-one fireplaces. The Eaton mansion stood on the north side of Elm Street, about halfway between Church and State streets where Orange Street was later cut through. Of New Haven's first governor, Cotton Mather wrote: "Mr. Eaton being yearly and ever chosen their Governor, it was the Admiration of all Spectators to behold the Discretion, the Gravity, the Equity with which he managed all their Public Affairs. . . . He was the Guide of the Blind, the Staff of the Lame, the Helper of the Widow and the Orphan and all the Distressed; . . . on the side he was the Terror of Evil Doers." He served as governor from 1639 until his death in 1658.

# From Trading Post to Statehood

"QUINUTUCQUET"—the aboriginal name of "the Land of Steady Habits"—has been translated as "upon the Long Tidal River," but this sloping plain drained by New England's greatest inland waterway lay, in the beginning, beneath a primordial sea.

When at last the waters retreated, new geologic pressures began to reshape the state, and over its first thousands of years, Connecticut had its ups and downs. The old sea bed was folded into mountain ranges which long ages of erosion planed away. Some sections of the new plain then sunk into hollows, and these were filled with gravel and sand by streams coursing over the land. During the Age of Dinosaurs, footprints and fossils were pressed into this softer terrain.

Eruptions from beneath the surface rock sent lava flowing over the land, and then new mountain-making forces tilted the sandstones and hardened lava into a new rough landscape, which was again flattened by eons of erosion, creating a new plain near sea level throughout southern New England.

Then came the Ice Age to carve the state into its present geologic shape. For hundreds of thousands of years, the ice sheet ground at the plain beneath it, shifting soil and loose stones, snapping off slabs of bedrock, polishing, scratching, and gouging. Gradually, the top and front of the ice cap began to melt, but even when southern New England had thawed out, floods continued to pour down from the north. The water brought Connecticut a new layer of topsoil from Massachusetts, New Hampshire, and Vermont to replace that carried by the ice to Long Island. It also deposited glacial debris, which formed such quaintly named geologic features as the "drumlins" in Storrs (the present site of the University of Connecticut) and sunken "kettles" elsewhere in the state. The shifting of debris changed the courses of rivers too; in preglacial times, the Farmington River flowed south into New Haven harbor, but glacial deposits diverted it so that it now empties into the Connecticut at Windsor, near one of the state's first three settlements. Another beneficiary of the end of the Ice Age was the state's coastline; its deep bays, inlets, rocky islands, estuaries, and tidal rivers were at least partly caused by the huge floods from melting ice, which elevated the sea level and shaped a new coast.

How long the land rested unpeopled after the ice melted away has not been firmly established, but the first inhabitants of Connecticut were tribes of the Algonkian group, who probably came from the west in the great eastward and southern migrations that had begun perhaps 40,000 years ago when the glaciers lowered the sea to create a land bridge from Siberia to Alaska. The early settlers of Connecticut were both hunters and farmers, and lived mostly in family-size wigwams, although the River Indians are said to have constructed longhouses that stretched quonset-style as long as sixty feet. From the land, the Algonkian tribes took wild berries, mushrooms, beech, hickory, and chestnuts, acorns, sunflower seeds, maple syrup and sugar, and such game as moose, deer, beaver, turkey, duck; from the rivers, lakes and seas, they took all types of fish, clams, lobsters, even whales. Their main crops were corn, beans, and tobacco.

The men hunted, and the women farmed. There were wars among the Algonkian tribes, and sometimes fights with the fierce Mohawks who lived along the eastern and northern borders of Vermont. When the first white men came to Connecticut in the early 1600s, there were perhaps 6,000 Indians in the state, mostly living east of the river. Chief among these were four main groups: the Nipmunk, the Pequot-Mohegan, the Sequin or 'River Indians,' and the Matabesec or Wappinger Confederacy.

The first white man on record to sail up the Connecticut was the Dutch sea captain Adriaen Block, who found a fortified Indian village, not far from where Hartford now stands, in 1614. But a permanent Dutch trading post was not set up until 1633. The English settlements at Plymouth and Massachusetts Bay knew nothing of the land to the southwest until 1631, when a small band of Podunks came to Plymouth to suggest opening up trade with them in the Connecticut Valley. The Podunks (or Mohegans in some sources) were looking to the white men as protectors against the Pequots who had driven them from their hunting grounds; a similar offer to the Dutch had been rejected.

In the summer of 1632, a group from Plymouth led by Edward Winslow visited the river and found it "a fine place," predicting that "the most certainty of profit would be by keeping a house there to receive the trade when it came down out of the inland."

The following year, 1633, was to see the first settlements in the state. In June, the Dutch built a small house on land bought from the Pequots and fortified it with two small cannons. Then in September, Capt. William Holmes of Plymouth sailed past Dutch Point to where the Farmington flowed into the Connecticut and set up a frame house to serve as a trading post on land bought from the Mohegans in what is now Windsor. In the same year, John Oldham of Watertown and three others explored the Connecticut Valley and discovered "many very desireable places upon the same river, fit to receive many hundred inhabitants." And the migration from Massachusetts Bay began.

In 1634, a large party from Watertown settled at Pyquag (now Wethersfield). Because the first crop in the valley was planted in Wethersfield, it claims to be the oldest town in the state, while Windsor's claim of seniority is based on the construction of the first permanent building in the summer of 1635 by settlers from Dorchester.

THIS MURAL by Walter R. Korder at Hartford's Municipal Building, done in 1934, depicts the Dutch in their trading post in Hartford watching the long boat coming ashore from the English ship sailing up the Connecticut River. Its caption reads: "July 1634: Six Scouts of the Bay, sent to discover the Connecticut River, reach the House of Hope at Suckiaug, new Hartford." (HC)

THIS SKELETON, found in a shallow grave in South Glastonbury, is believed to be the last remains of a Narragansett Indian shot during King Philip's War. A Glastonbury doctor who examined the remains in 1959 deduced that the Indian was a runner who died of peritonitis which developed from his wound. (HC)

That October, fifty persons from New Town, or Cambridge, settled at Suckiaug (Hartford) close to the Dutch trading post, and the Rev. Thomas Hooker and his flock followed the Old Bay Path westward the following spring. Land in Cambridge where Hooker had arrived two years earlier was becoming scarce, and Hooker disagreed with some of the policies of the older Puritan leaders there. And by most accounts, the place was overcrowded with leaders and ministers anyway.

From the time of the early settlements, Connecticut's early history was to be dominated by the shaping of the nation's first constitutional government on the one hand, and by the decimation of the native Indians on the other.

The principal antagonism in the 1630s was between the English and the Pequots, headed until their final destruction by a sachem known as Sassacus. Allied with the settlers in this war of attrition was the Indian, Uncas, known through his namesake in James Fennimore Cooper's *The Last of the Mohicans.* By the standards of all but contemporary U.S. history, Uncas was a noble savage, but he can hardly be regarded as a leader in the cause of Indians' rights.

Sassacus, on the other hand, sought to forestall the encroachments of the white man by seeking a treaty with the Narragansetts of Rhode Island, but this was blocked by the intercession of Roger Williams of the Providence Plantation, exiled from Massachusetts Bay, but still helpful to his former enemies. The bad blood between Pequots and settlers began in 1633 with a massacre or accidental explosion which took the lives of a boatload of traders sailing up river under the command of a "dissolute" Captain Stone. An uneasy peace prevailed for three years, however, until the murder of John Oldham by Indians on Block Island in 1636.

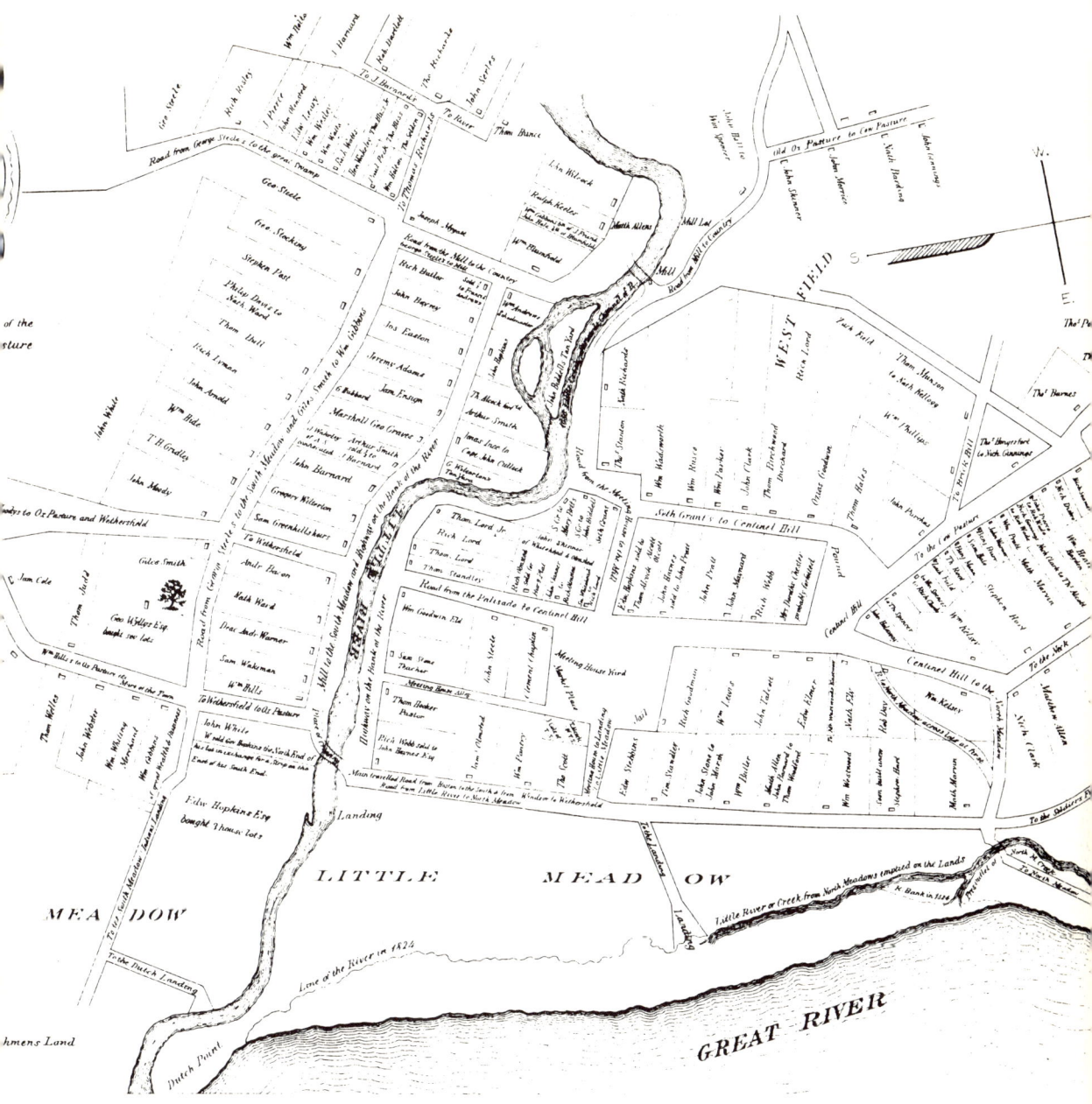

THIS COPY OF A 1640 map shows how Hartford was laid out less than ten years after its settlement by the English colonists. The road along the river—approximately where an interstate highway now runs—says: "Main travelled Road from Boston to the South & from Windsor to Wethersfield Road from Little River to North Meadow." The Little River later was called the Park River, or the Hog River, and is now mostly underground in the downtown area. In the lower right-hand corner of the map is Dutch Point, site of the original Dutch trading post in 1633, and "Dutchmens Land." The house of Thomas Hooker was to the right of the Little River, one lot west of the "Main travelled Road." (HC)

[ 15 ]

The first responses by white troops under John Endicott were ineffectual, and there was little bloodshed on either side. But the Pequots were stirred up. "You have come to raise a nest of wasps about our ears, and then you will flee away," Endicott was told by Lt. Lion Gardiner, commander of a fort at Saybrook at the mouth of the Connecticut. The prediction was prophetic; Pequot braves captured and tortured men at Gardiner's garrison and two men who came ashore from a boat near the fort. Throughout the winter of 1636-37, the fort was virtually under siege. At Wethersfield, 200 Pequots also fell upon the settlement, killing four women and six men and carrying off two girls (who were later returned through negotiations by the Dutch).

Then on May 1, 1637, the settlers took action. The Connecticut General Court, the colony's legislative body, met in extra session in Hartford and voted to carry on a defensive war. They raised an army of ninety men—probably close to half the adult males in Hartford, Windsor, and Wethersfield, and equipped them with arms and supplies under the command of Capt. John Mason, an experienced soldier who had fought the Dutch in the Netherlands. Uncas provided an additional seventy warriors, and with help on the way from Massachusetts Bay, the war party set forth down the river on May 10, 1637.

After sailing down the river and eastward into Rhode Island, Mason's troops doubled back into Connecticut. Then on a morning in early June, they rose before dawn and crept up Pequot Hill in West Mystic. They entered the sleeping fortification and began putting Indians to the sword until the encampment was awake. Then the colonists set the Pequot fort aflame. Capt. John Underhill, who had been sent with nineteen men from Massachusetts later wrote: "Many courageous fellows . . . fought most desperately through the pallisades so that they scorched and burned with the very flame . . . and so perished valiantly . . . many being in the fort, both men, women and children. Others, forced out, came in troops . . . 20 or 30 at a time, which our soldiers received and entertained with the point of a sword." At least 400 or 500 Pequots were killed. Sassacus and a few hundred of his warriors attacked from nearby Fort Hill, but the English made it back to their boats. From that time forward, Sassacus lost his support, and most of the remaining Pequots were killed in a swamp fight in Fairfield in July, though their leader himself escaped—only to be beheaded by the Mohawks from whom he and the remnants of his tribe had sought sanctuary.

In the years that followed, the English negotiated a treaty of "perpetual peace" between the Narragansetts and the Mohegans, but after the machinations of Uncas with the River tribes, there was war again. Miantinomo, chief of the Narragansetts, was killed by Uncas' brother after the United Colonies of New England, in their first official meeting in 1643, decided to hand the captive Indian back to his enemies. Hostilities between the Narragansetts and the Mohegans continued until 1658, when the Narragansetts, the Nehantics, and the Massachusetts tribes invaded Mohegan country and were repulsed.

But from the death of Sassacus, in 1637, until 1679 there were nearly forty years of peace between the white settlers and the Indians. As the settlers took over more and more of the Indians' hunting grounds, however, the natives rallied under Metacom or "King Philip" of the Wampanoags, who sought to unite all the Indians in New England. In June 1675, Metacom attacked Swansea, near Mount Hope, Rhode Island, killing nine and

"HOOKER'S EMIGRATION TO CONNECTICUT" is depicted in a nineteenth-century engraving. The party of the Rev. Thomas Hooker, Hartford's first leader, came from Massachusetts Bay in the spring of 1735, along the Old Bay Path. Mrs. Hooker was carried in the litter.

wounding seven. None of the battles in what has become known as King Philip's War was fought in Connecticut, but men from the state fought and died in the "great swamp fight" in December 1675, which saw the decimation of the Narragansetts in a massacre that echoed the destruction of the Pequots at Mystic. By July 1676, a century before the Declaration of Independence, Indian resistance was dead in southern New England, and the noble Metacom was dead, shot in a swamp near Mount Hope by an Indian ally.

The relative peace that had prevailed between the Pequot wars and the final fight against the New England alliance allowed Connecticut's new settlers to build new towns under new ways of government. As early as 1639, Hartford and its neighbors to the north and south, Windsor and Wethersfield, on the west bank of the river, had adopted the Fundamental Orders, sometimes described as the first practical Constitution. The document, drafted mainly by Roger Ludlow under the inspiration of Thomas Hooker's sermon of May 31, 1638, was based on these three doctrines as enunciated by the pastor-leader:

"*Doctrine I.* That the choice of public magistrates belongs to the people by God's own allowance."

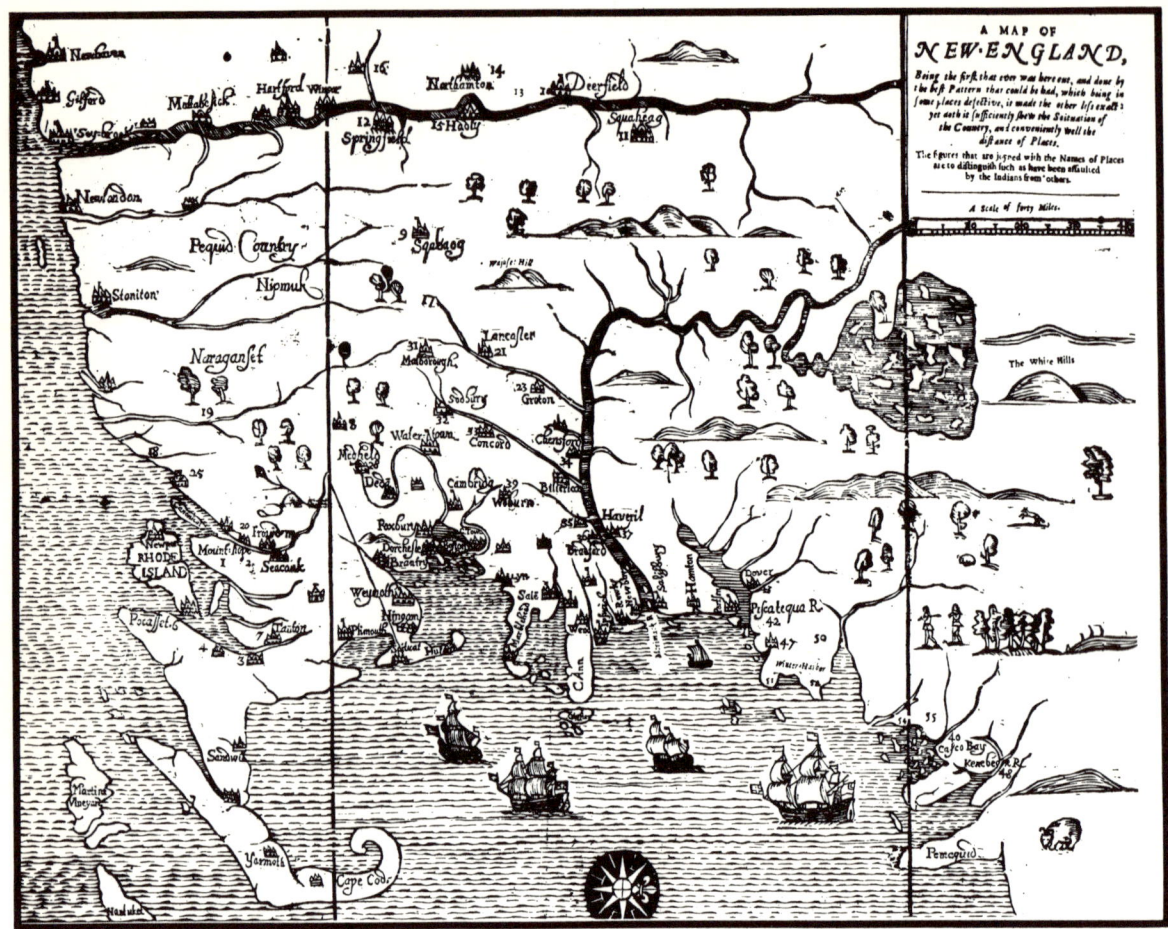

CONNECTICUT is the upper left-hand corner, with Newhaven, Gilford, Say-brook, New London, and Stoniton along the coastline and Mattabesick, Hartford, and Winsor inland in this 1677 map of New England, in which north is right.

"*Doctrine II:* The privilege of election which belongs unto the people must not be exercised according to their humors, but according to the blessed will of God."

"*Doctrine III:* That they who have the power to appoint officers and magistrates, it is in their power also to set the bounds and limitations of the power and place unto which they call them."

As early as 1636, a general court had been held; the Fundamental Orders—providing for a "publick state or commonwealth"—made this court the supreme authority, with deputies from the towns working in concert. Until the Constitution of 1818 replaced the Fundamental Orders and the Charter of 1662, the legislative body continued to dominate the executive and the judicial branches.

After the Hartford area towns, the second settlement in the state was at Saybrook, by order of an English company of lords and gentlemen. In charge of this enterprise were

John Winthrop, Jr., son of the governor of Massachusetts Bay; his aides were Col. George Fenwick and Capt. Lion Gardiner, whose son David was the first white child born in Connecticut, on April 29, 1636. At first the settlement did not thrive except as a fort and trading post, and in 1644, Fenwick sold his rights to the Connecticut Colony in Hartford.

That was six years after the state's third settlement, which was to become a major city in the state and to share the capitol with Hartford. Quinnipiac, later New Haven, was settled in 1638 under the Rev. John Davenport, a Puritan minister from London, and Theophilas Eaton, a prominent merchant of his congregation. The land was bought from a local sachem named Montowese, for 23 coats, 12 spoons, 24 knives, 12 hatchets, scissors, and some hoes and porringers. New Haven had no patents until it, too, was absorbed into the Connecticut Colony in 1665. New Haven's government, run by "seven pillars" headed by Eaton, the elected magistrate, stipulated that "church members only shall be free burgesses, and that they only shall choose magistrates and officers among themselves to have the power of transacting all the publique civill affaires of this Plantation. . . ." Strict old-testamentarian blue laws were in effect, and these included the death penalty for a child over sixteen who struck or cursed a parent, a ban on smoking except in a room of a public house, and punishment by branding, whipping, or banishment for Quakers.

In 1643, New Haven was extended to include Milford, Guilford, and Stamford, but the new colony had its problems. A shipping venture died in its maiden voyage, when the "Great Shippe" or "Wonder-Working Providence" went down at sea with several leading

THE LAYOUT OF NEW HAVEN in the mid-1700s is shown in this map. In the center of the "nine squares" is the New Haven Green which remains to the present pretty much as it looked in the early 1800s. At the time this map was drawn, the Second Meeting House, built in 1668, stood in the middle of the green, and the first Yale College House faces the green in the upper righthand corner. (NHR)

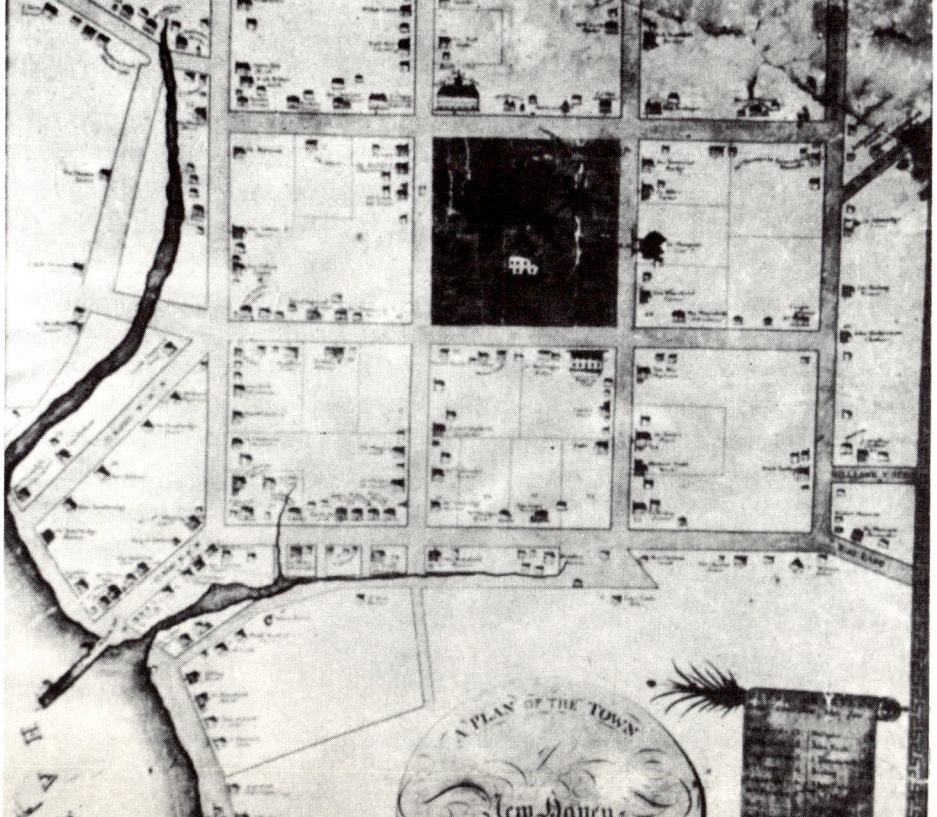

citizens aboard. It reappeared only as a legendary "phantom ship" in the skies over New Haven.

None of the three original settlements in Connecticut possessed a charter that would stand up to much legal scrutiny. New Haven and Hartford, or Connecticut, had merely bought land from the Indians; Saybrook had a deed of conveyance from Warwick, but there was no evidence that the original patent had been executed. When Charles II was restored to the throne in 1660, the Colony recognized quickly that a crisis was at hand. John Winthrop, Jr., who had been elected governor in 1657 and reelected in 1659, went overseas to straighten out matters, and, in fact, somehow managed to obtain a royal charter which placed the king's approval on the system of government already in existence. The charter set forth boundaries—from Massachusetts to the Sound and from Narragansett Bay to the Pacific—which had the effect of annexing New Haven into the more liberal and democratic Connecticut Colony whether it wanted to join or not.

But before New Haven finally succumbed and threw in with the Colony in preference to being annexed by the Duke of York's Anglican Colony, the celebrated incident of the "judges cave" caused considerable excitement. William Goffe and Edward Whalley, who had both signed the death warrant of Charles I, had fled to Boston and from there to Davenport's house in New Haven. While the agents pursuing them were delayed at every turn, Goffe and Whalley fled to a mill outside of town, and then were hidden in a cave on West Rock where the "regicides" stayed for nearly a month.

During the remainder of the 1600s, the sovereignty of Connecticut was twice threatened by Maj. Edmund Andros, an English soldier and aristocrat then serving as governor of New York, A year after his appointment in 1674, Andros demanded that all land west of the Connecticut River be surrendered to him under a new royal patent. The 1662 charter was cited, but on July 8, Andros brought several armed sloops before Saybrook, only to sail off four days later after a show of force by the colonists there.

Then, in 1687, came the famous Charter Oak incident. Andros had come to Hartford from Boston with a retinue of 75 men. On a morning in late October, he and his party met with Gov. Robert Treat at the meeting house. At the meeting, Andros ordered the King's orders of annexation read, and may even have demanded the surrender of the charter. Governor Treat responded with a long recital of the trials of the young colony. As the autumnal darkness dimmed the room, candles were lighted.

"The important affair was debated and kept in suspense," says an early history, "until the evening, when the charter was brought and laid upon the table where the assembly was sitting. By this time great numbers of people were assembled. . . . The lights were instantly extinguished, and one Captain Wadsworth of Hartford, in the most silent and secret manner, carried off the charter and secreted it in a large hollow tree. The candles were officiously relighted; but the patent was gone, and no discovery could be made of it, or of the person who had conveyed it away." The Andros government took over anyway, but only for two years.

During the century between the granting of the charter and the Revolution, Connecticut engaged in border disputes with its neighbors, burned witches, and participated in the

YALE COLLEGE looked like this after completion of its first two buildings, the College, built in 1750, and the Chapel, built in 1761. This is the earliest view of Yale, printed by Daniel Bowen from a woodcut in 1785. The students near Pres. Ezra Stiles, in front of the Chapel, have removed their hats, a time-honored custom at Yale. (HC)

colonial wars. In 1690, Fitz-John Winthop led an unsuccessful expedition against Montreal, and twenty years later, about 300 Connecticut militiamen were among those who captured Port Royal during Queen Anne's War. The colony also contributed fighting men to the force that took Louisburg in 1745, and during the French and Indian War, it wavered between cooperation and obstruction.

The early eighteenth century saw the creation of Connecticut's most famous institution of higher learning, and the beginning of a rapid population growth which made the colony one of the most densely populated at the start of the Revolution, with nearly 200,000 souls. The Collegiate School, later to be called Yale University, received its charter to provide "the training up of youthful citizens for publik employment in Church & State" from the General Assembly in 1701. The school held its first classes in Saybrook. More than sixty graduates passed through the school's courses during the time it was in Saybrook, but in 1716, the trustees voted to move to New Haven after that city outbid all others in providing funds and land. Its first building there was on a half acre at the edge of town. Early gifts to the young college included 500 pounds from the colony to pay for construction of a "college house," and the government continued to provide funds which enabled the construction of the Old Brick Row.

The name Yale came to the college through its first major private benefaction in 1718 of nine bales of goods, with 562 pounds, 12 shillings, and 417 books from the East India merchant and Madras governor, Elihu Yale, whose grandmother had married one of the founders of New Haven, Theophilius Eaton.

In addition to being the site of Connecticut's first and, for many years, only college, New Haven became the colony's largest city during the eighteenth century. In the 1756 census, it was outstripped by Middletown, founded on the Connecticut below Hartford in 1651, and by Norwich, founded at the head of the Thames River in eastern Connecticut in 1659. But by the 1774 census, New Haven had grown from 5,085 in 1756 to 8,295. (Norwich had jumped too, from 5,540 in 1756 to 7,327, but Middletown was the only one of the colony's major cities to show a population drop—from 5,664 in 1756 to 4,878 in 1774). By 1774, Hartford stood only eighth in population with barely 5,000 residents. Besides, New Haven and Norwich, Farmington, New London, Stratford, Stonington, and Woodbury stood ahead of it in size. But no one town was large enough to stand out as a real metropolis and dominant force, as were Boston and Philadelphia.

In the years before the Revolution, farming was the main occupation of the colony. Corn was the principal crop, with rye, oats, barley, flax, and hemp also grown along with such vegetables as beans, squash, peas, and pumpkins. Early industries included gristmills, cloth manufacture, iron making, clock building, shipping, and ship building. And the Yankee trader began to develop his reputation for shrewd and hard dealings.

The years before the Revolution also saw the rise of the Anglican Church to stand with the long dominant Congregationalists, and the start of the first newspapers. The *Connecticut Gazette,* in New Haven, was the first in 1755, the *New-London Summary* followed in 1758 (succeeded in 1763 by the *Gazette*), and then in 1764, the *Connecticut Courant* began publishing in Hartford. (Today, as *The Hartford Courant,* it claims to be the oldest American newspaper in continuous circulation.) Though at first politically moderate, the *Courant* became recognizably anti-British; it called the Boston Tea Party an ACCIDENT!! By July 1774, two years before the Declaration of Independence, the *Courant* was full of revolutionary news.

The issue of July 12, 1774, reported that "We hear from Canaan, that on the 21st of June last, a large number of inhabitants of that and neighboring towns assembled together at the sign of the brazen bull and raised a standard of Liberty, 78 feet high, and fixed a scarlet flag on the top, 15 feet in length with the words LIBERTY and PROPERTY inscribed in Large Capitals."

In October 1774, the town of Mansfield passed the so-called "Mansfield Declaration of Independence," and the October session of the Assembly heard Gov. Jonathan Trumbull urge a commitment to the "invaluable blessings of freedom contained and secured in and by our Civil Constitution." Extra training was ordered for the militia and supplies of powder, balls, and flints built up. Like the other colonies, Connecticut was moving toward war.

RIPLEY'S COFFEE HOUSE was a popular Hartford institution in the 1700s. It stood on State Street until 1826, when the United States Hotel was built on the site. This is how it looked in an advertisement in 1823 when a third story had been added.

HARTFORD'S FIRST STATE HOUSE was this wood frame structure which stood from 1719 to 1796 on Main Street, the present site of the Old State House designed by Bullfinch. It was moved in 1796 and ended its days as a tenement house before it was demolished in 1910. (HC)

"THE 17TH-CENTURY TAVERN" was moved from its original site in Brookfield to 105 West Wooster Street in Danbury in 1918. Many distinguished guests were entertained at the tavern when it stood in Brookfield, on the old post road, shown below by the coach at left. Among the guests was Jerome Bonaparte, brother of Napoleon. (HC)

THE ACADIAN HOUSE in Guilford, seen here as it looked in 1931, was used to house destitute Acadian peasants set ashore in Guilford from a British ship in the autumn of 1755, after the destruction of Grand Pre, Nova Scotia. The house was built in 1670 by Joseph Clay.

When a postrider carried in news of the "shot heard round the world" on April 19, 1775, Connecticut quickly mobilized. Col. Israel Putnam was plowing his farm in Pomfret when the postrider arrived with the news of the Battle of Lexington. It is said he left his farm to warn local militia officers and to depart for Cambridge so hurriedly that he left his team yoked in the field. In all, nearly 3600 men followed Putnam to Boston. Among their leaders was Capt. Benedict Arnold, who led the Second Company, Governor's Foot Guard, into the fight despite a cold reaction from New Haven officials.

Arnold was also instrumental in planning the seizure of the rundown Fort Ticonderoga from the British, suggesting that its cannons could easily be captured, and then marching at the head of the troops that took the fort in early May, though Green Mountain Boy Ethan Allen was in charge, overruling Arnold's ambitions to lead himself. Early in the war, Colonel Putnam and Captain Arnold became Connecticut's two leading military leaders. It was Putnam who gave the order, "Don't fire until you see the white of their eyes," as first in command at Bunker Hill. And Arnold displayed a dashing heroism during

NATHAN HALE taught in this New London schoolhouse from March 1774 until July 1755, when he enlisted. The schoolhouse, now restored, was built in 1774.

THE DECLARATION OF INDEPENdence appeared as a news story in the *Connecticut Courant* (on page 2, in custom with putting in reports as they were received) in July of 1776.

PHILADELPHIA.
In CONGRESS, July 4, 1776.
A DECLARATION
By the REPRESENTATIVES of the
UNITED STATES OF AMERICA,
In GENERAL CONGRESS ASSEMBLED.
WHEN in the Courfe of human Events, it becomes neceffary for one People to diffolve the political Bands which have connected them with another, and to affume among the Powers of the Earth, the feparate and equal Station to which the Laws of Nature and Of Nature's God entitle them, a decent Refpect to the Opinion of Mankind requires that they fhould declare the Caufe which impel them to the Separation.

[ 25 ]

CONNECTICUT had a great number of its present towns in 1777 during the Revolution, when this map was made.

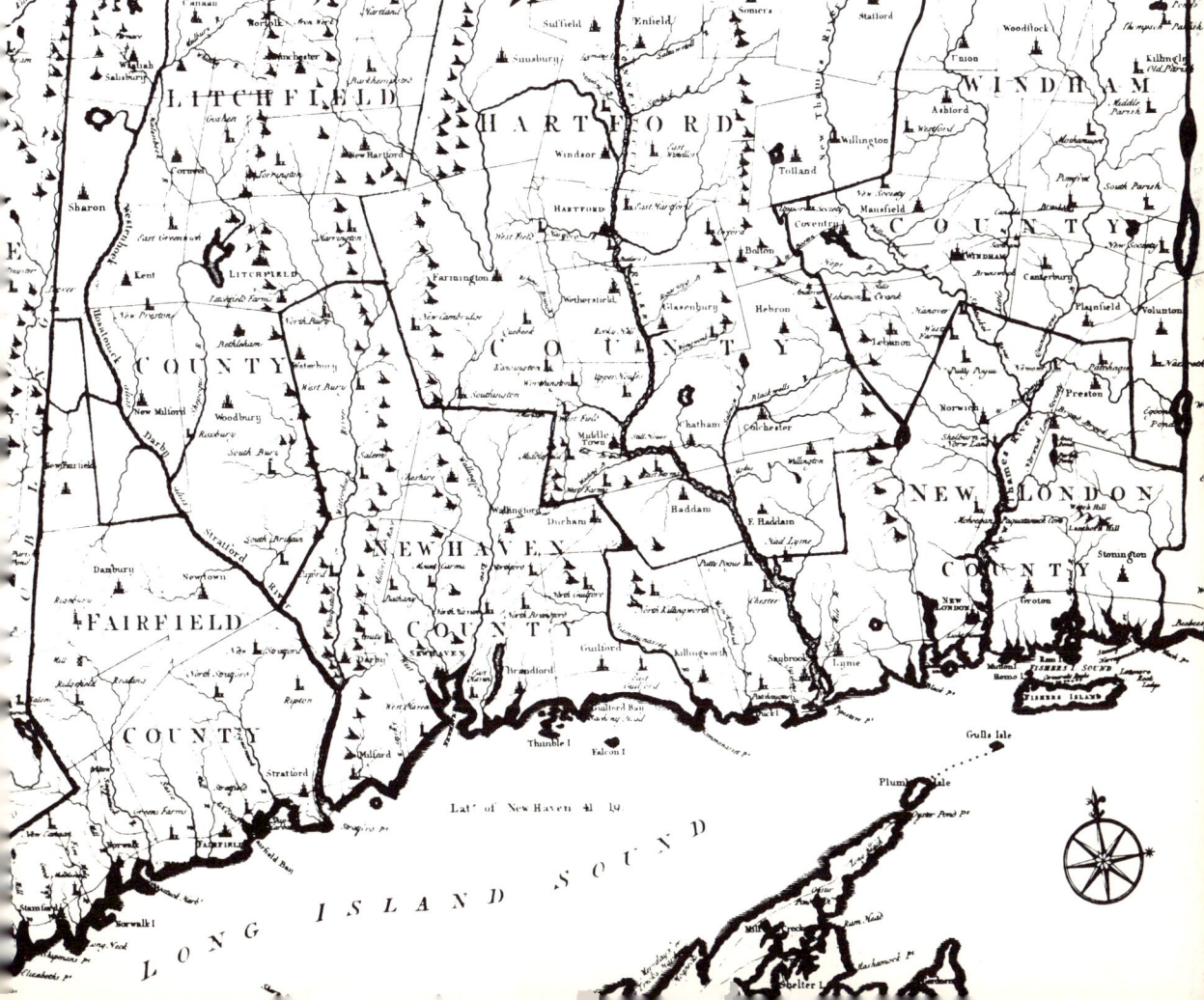

ISRAEL PUTNAM distinguished himself as commander of the American troops at the Battle of Bunker Hill, but later in the Revolution his military skills seemed to decline. General Washington removed Putnam from battlefield command after he was outflanked in the Battle of Long Island. He retired to his farm in 1779 after a paralytic stroke. This painting by Alonzo Chappel shows "Old Put" eluding pursuers. (HC)

THE NAME OF BENEDICT ARNOLD is today synonymous with betrayal of one's country, but early in the Revolution, Arnold was one of the ablest officers in the Continental Army and a flamboyant, courageous hero. (HC)

an attack at Danbury in April 1777, and in the battles of Saratoga in September of that year. In the first Battle of Saratoga, at Freeman's Farm, Arnold galloped into the center of the fray, was cheered by the troops, and answered with braggadocio: "Now come on, boys. If the day is long enough, we'll have them all in Hell before the night."

But as the war kept on, both Putnam and Arnold fell from grace, though Putnam's fall had nothing to do with disloyalty, but with old age. It was simply that "Old Put"—made a major general and field commander by Washington—had allowed himself to be flanked by the British in the Battle of Long Island in the spring of 1776.

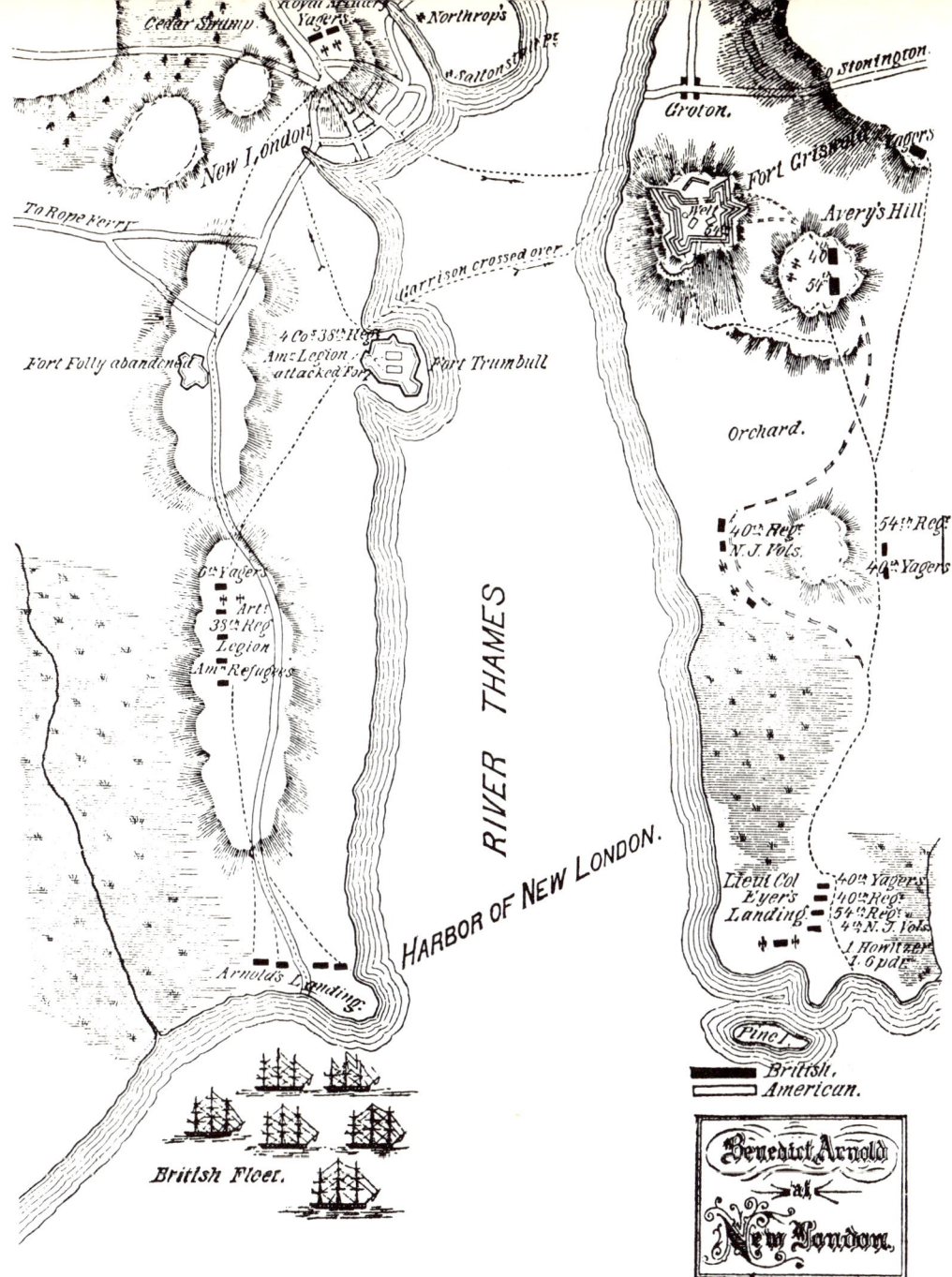

*Compiled and Drawn by Col. Carrington.*

THE ONLY MAJOR BATTLE of the Revolution to occur on Connecticut soil was a British attack on New London and Groton led by Benedict Arnold on September 6, 1781. This map depicts Arnold's landing on the New London Bank of the Thames River, and that of Lieutenant-Colonel Eyer on the Groton side. Arnold's men easily overcame resistance at Fort Trumbull and set fire to New London, burning homes, wharves, and warehouses containing loot of American privateers which operated out of the port. Fort Griswold was harder to take, but finally the British overran the fort after the death of thier commander. Col. William Ledyard, who commanded Fort Griswold, was put to death by his own sword.

[ 27 ]

Arnold's betrayal of the American cause became known in September 1780, in time to thwart his plan of delivering West Point to the British, but a year later he led a division of British troops against the seaport of New London—the worst attack on Connecticut during the war. Connecticut's troops under Col. William Ledyard bravely held Fort Griswold for a time, killing 40 British and wounding 100. When the fort was taken, Ledyard was brutally slain with his own sword, and an ammunition wagon carrying wounded crashed out of control, maiming and killing many of its passengers. The British then put New London to the torch, leaving 65 houses, 31 stores and warehouses, 18 shops, 20 barns, nine public buildings, and a dozen ships in ruins.

Despite the horror of the New London raid, Connecticut was ravaged but little during the eight years of fighting. Between the attack on Danbury in 1777 and the New London assault in 1781, there was a small raid on the salt works in Greenwich, and a heavier assault on New Haven, which served as a base for attacks by American privateers on British commerce. Among the defenders of New Haven were members of the Governor's Guard, volunteers, and Yale students. The British advance was hindered for a time by Napthali Daggett, the retired president of Yale, then in his seventies, who enjoyed a peppery exchange with the invaders before he was taken prisoner.

Connecticut provided hundreds of fighting men for the Revolution, despite pockets of Toryism, especially in the western part of the state. There were heroes among the patriots: Capt. Nathan Hale, a young Yale graduate who uttered the famous "I only regret that I have but one life to lose for my country" before he was hanged as a spy on September 21, 1776, on Long Island; Col. Return Jonathan Meigs of Middletown who led a daring raid on Sag Harbor, Long Island, from Sachem's Head, Guildford, in May 1777, and took a leading role in the victory at Stony Point in July 1779; and Col. Thomas Knowlton of Knowlton's Rangers, an able leader killed in the Battle of Harlem in the spring of 1776.

But Connecticut's other crucial importance to the War of Independence was in the supplies it provided. Salt works on the coast replaced imports, and powder mills were built at East Hartford, Windham, New Haven, Glastonbury, Stratford, and Salisbury. Gun-makers stepped up production in Windham, Mansfield, and Goshen, and the Salisbury iron foundry turned out cannons. The Revolution, in fact, probably provided the start of Connecticut's armaments industries.

THIS ANCIENT "PROSPECTIVE VIEW of old Newgate, Connecticut's state prison" says, "the subterranean vault over which this place was built was wrought about the middle of the 17th Century for the purpose of obtaining copper ore." Prisoners worked the mines during the Revolution. (HC)

# Growing with a New Nation

WITH THE EIGHT LONG YEARS of war and deprivation past, Connecticut and the other former colonies could again begin building, as their leaders worked to find new forms of government.

On the state level, one of the first actions of the Assembly was to create the first five cities in the state: New Haven, New London, Hartford, Middletown, and Norwich. On the federal level, Connecticut sent a delegation of three to the interstate convention in Philadelphia in May 1887, and the Assembly chose Oliver Ellsworth, William Samuel Johnson, and Roger Sherman as its delegates. Their most famous contribution to the convention was the Connecticut Compromise, providing for equal representation in the Senate and proportional in the House of Representatives. Connecticut became the fifth state to ratify the new Constitution after five days of debate at the Meeting House of the First Society in Hartford.

Through the early part of the new century, Federalists dominated Connecticut politics, but Jeffersonian Republicans began to develop an effective opposition, campaigning for a new Constitution, and for an end to unfair taxation and extravagance in local government. The Federalists' opposition to Jefferson and to his successor, James Madison, was clearly demonstrated at the start of the War of 1812, when the anti-Jeffersonian *Courant* called the declaration of war "dreadful tidings," while the Republican *American Mercury*, a newer Hartford paper, called the war "just, honorable and necessary."

In the second year of the war, the state was blockaded. (An intrepid Norwich citizen sought to torpedo a British ship using perhaps the state's first submarine, a crude forerunner to the nuclear giants built at Groton's Electric Boat today.) There were almost constant fears of a British landing, but only two attacks—a raid by about 200 British sailors and marines on Pettipaug Point in Essex, where 20 small vessels and a sail loft were destroyed in April, 1914, and a more serious attack on Stonington that August when two landing attempts were repulsed before the British fleet poured roughly 60 tons of metal into the seacost town.

If the residents of Stonington acquitted themselves with heroism in August, the Hartford Convention in December hardly gave the capital city a reputation for patriotism. Delegates from Massachusetts, Rhode Island, and Connecticut, and unofficial representatives from Vermont and New Hampshire held secret sessions at the old State House in Hartford, giving Republicans the notion that conspiracy was afoot. It wasn't—the convention was essentially a Federalist power play, but the news of Jackson's victory in the Battle of New Orleans and of peace came hard on the heels of the convention's recommendations to Madison, and instead of undermining Madison, the convention served mainly to discredit Federalism.

By 1818, a Republican-Episcopalian fusion party called the Tolerationists had elected a governor and both houses of the Assembly, and in August a Constitutional Convention began at the State House in Hartford. The new document, which superceded the Charter of 1662, provided for clear separation of powers, new election laws, annual elections, and legislative sessions, alternating between the capitols in Hartford and New Haven, and disestablishment of the Congregational Church.

The post-Revolutionary period and the early part of the new century saw the expansion of colonial industries and the creation of new businesses that would continue to grow even into the modern era. The years after the War of Independence were good ones for the shipping business and inspired the creation of the state's first banks, the Hartford Bank and the Union Bank of New London, both founded in 1792. The blockades of the War of 1812 provided a serious setback for shipping from which the industry never recovered, but the 1800s gave another maritime industry strength: whaling. New London became the third among American whaling ports in the 1840s and 1850s, ranking behind only New Bedford and Nantucket.

Coinciding with whaling was the state's shipbuilding industry, centering in Mystic, on the site of the present Mystic Seaport maritime museum, where many of America's most celebrated packets and clipper ships were built. Steamships were also built at Portland and Fairhaven, following the early lead of John Fitch, a South Windsor native who completed the first model of the steamboat in 1785. Steamboat transportation was common in Connecticut during the early part of the 1800s, which also saw the construction of the Enfield and Farmington canals.

Two of what were to become the state's most important industries were both begun shortly before the turn of the century. In 1798, Eli Whitney, already the inventor of the cotton gin, went into the gun business, and on February 8, 1794, the first printed insurance policy was drawn by the Hartford firm of Sanford & Wadsworth, providing 800 pounds worth of protection for the house of William Imlay of Hartford.

Whitney's early arms manufacturing plant near East Rock in Hamden was one of the first to produce machined interchangeable parts, as the inventor himself demonstrated in January 1801 in Washington, D.C., in pleading for time to produce rifles he had promised but not yet delivered. There were other early important arms makers as well: Simon North of Middletown began the first major pistol factory in America, which gave way to

NOAH WEBSTER, born in West Hartford in 1758, is best known today as the author of the first American dictionary, but his biggest seller was the Blue-Backed Speller, published in Hartford in 1783. The title page of the speller, *A Grammatical Institute of the English Language* is shown at right. The *American Dictionary of the English Language* was published by Webster in 1828. (HC)

A
**Grammatical Inſtitute,**
OF THE
ENGLISH LANGUAGE,
COMPRISING,
An eaſy, conciſe, and ſyſtematic Method of
EDUCATION,
Deſigned for the Uſe of *Engliſh* Schools
In *AMERICA.*

IN THREE PARTS.

PART I.
CONTAINING,
A new and accurate Standard of Pronunciation.

By NOAH WEBSTER, A. M.

*Uſus eſt Norma Loquendi.*   CICERO.

*HARTFORD:*
PRINTED BY HUDSON & GOODWIN,
FOR THE AUTHOR.

THE LITCHFIELD LAW SCHOOL, founded by Judge Tapping Reeve in 1784, was the first law school in the nation. Judge Reeve conducted the school until 1820, when it was taken over by Judge James Gould who ran it until the school closed in 1833. More than one thousand students were graduated from the school, among them John C. Calhoun of Abbeville, South Carolina. The building is shown before its restoration and afterwards. It was moved from its original site in 1849 and allowed to deteriorate until 1929 when it was purchased by the Litchfield Historical Society and moved back to its original location in the yard of Judge Reeve's home on South Street.

OYSTER HUTS, like the ones shown in this engraving made about 1800, stood on Milford Point in Milford. Long Island Sound was a rich source for fish and shellfish until modern times, when overdevelopment and pollution greatly reduced the state's fishing industry. (NHR)

the famed Colt's Patent Firearms Manufacturing Company in Hartford and its celebrated "Peacemaker;" Smith & Wesson pioneered improvements in repeating firearms in Norwich, and New Haven's Winchester Company evolved in part from the earlier firm.

From Sanford & Wadsworth's first policy, the insurance business began to expand. A number of Connecticut cities developed fire and marine companies before 1800, and the Hartford Fire Insurance Company was incorporated in 1810. Other companies were born throughout the early 1800s, as Hartford began on its way to becoming the nation's Insurance Capital.

Clock manufacturing was another early industry that has continued into the present; Eli Terry opened his first shop in Plymouth in 1793 and pioneered in the mass production of clocks there. By 1855, four Connecticut firms were producing a total of 400,000 rolled-brass clocks a year: Seth Thomas of Plymouth, William R. Gilbert of Winsted, E.N. Welch of Bristol (where the growth of this state industry is exhibited in a clock museum), and the New Haven Clock Company. Silver-making, a handcraft from 1700, entered the modern era in 1847 with the start of Rogers Brothers silver-plated flatware in Hartford; the firm was acquired by the Meriden Brittania Metal Co. in 1862, and the Rogers Brothers moved to Meriden where the firm is still located. The early 1800s also saw the birth of wool and cotton manufacturing, and the spread of Danbury's hat business, which counted 56 small hat shops in 1810.

The early 1800s and the start of the Industrial Revolution, with the growth of cities, created an increased demand for food, and commercial agriculture increased in the state. The subsistence farming that had been a way of life since the state's beginnings began to die away.

The 1830s saw the start of the Democratic party in Connecticut, though the Republicans continued to dominate well into the twentieth century. The decade also saw increasing opposition to slavery, although slavery was not abolished in the state until 1848. Two celebrated incidents in the 1830s showed the attitudes of the times.

BRANFORD CENTER'S meeting house, built between 1740 and 1744, had a steeple and clock added in 1803. All were removed in 1843. The small center, dominated by a church, was typical of Connecticut's towns in the early part of the nineteenth century.

The first was the case of Prudence Crandall, headmistress of a girls' school in the town of Canterbury, who accepted a black student, and then, confronted with backlash from the local townspeople, converted the school into an academy designed to teach black girls to become teachers themselves. Supported by abolitionist William Lloyd Garrison and the Rev. Samuel May, pastor of a Unitarian Church in nearby Brooklyn, Miss Crandall fought against boycotts by merchants who refused to sell her food and against the state legislature which passed a "Black Law" forbidding private schools for blacks unless authorized by the town. Her fight got her arrested, tried, and convicted; the conviction was overturned, but attacks on the school finally closed it in 1834.

THE ILL FEELING between the Federalists and the new Jeffersonian Republicans is graphically illustrated in this contemporary political cartoon. After an exchange of insults simmered for a few days in January 1798, Rep. Roger Griswold of Lyme, Connecticut, a Federalist, set upon Rep. Matthew Lyon of Vermont, a Republican, on the floor of the House of Representatives. Griswold, who later became a Connecticut governor, raises cane at right, while Lyon defends himself with fireplace tongs. Pres. John Adams subsequently offered Griswold the post of Secretary of War, but he declined. (HC)

The other case has a more contemporary echo. It concerned the mutiny aboard a Spanish slave ship, the *Amistad* (fictionalized in Herman Melville's *Benito Cereno,* and in Robert Lowell's play of the same name), and the subsequent trial of the leader of the mutineers in New Haven in 1939. The leader of the revolt was called Cinque (the name taken in the 1970s by the leader of the Symbionese Liberation Army), and the high point of his trial came when he took the stand and told, through an interpreter, how he had been forcibly taken away from his wife and children in Africa. The slaves were freed by the court, but years of legal hassles kept them in jail and in this country until they were finally returned to Sierra Leone in the 1840s.

Connecticut abolitionists played active roles in the underground railroad, helping fugitive slaves to escape to Canada. Perhaps the state's most famous abolitionist was John Brown, born in Torrington in 1800, but removed to Ohio with his family at the age of 5.

Though Brown's raid on Harper's Ferry in 1859 was condemned by both Republicans and Democrats in the 1860 local and national elections, the state registered a clear mandate for stopping the spread of slavery by giving Lincoln a landslide victory in the presidential vote.

In the four years of the Civil War, Connecticut again acted as a supply state as it had in the Revolution. Small arms were provided by Colt's and Sharps' Rifles in Hartford, by Whitney and Winchester in New Haven, and by Alsop and Savage in Middletown; the Hazard Powder Company of Enfield carried on production in 125 buildings; Connecticut's iron furnaces in Salisbury again forged armaments, this time the plate for ironclads; the Ames Company of Falls Village made sabres and swords, as did the Collins Company of Collinsville, the world's largest maker of axes and edged tools. The state's cotton and woolen mills boomed, and in the Naugatuck Valley at Waterbury, Ansonia, and Naugatuck, millions of brass buttons were made for Union uniforms. Then, as now, Connecticut prospered in wartime.

As for fighting units, Connecticut sent a regiment of cavalry, two of heavy artillery, three battalions of light artillery, and thirty regiments of infantry, two of them black. Altogether, about 55,000 Connecticut men fought in the bloody war with 20,000 casualties—among these 2,088 killed, missing, or fatally wounded, 2,801 dead from disease, and 689 perished in prison camps.

THIS ELI TERRY CLOCK with a pillar scrolltop case dates from 1814, and the printed notice pasted inside this model bears the name of Samuel Terry, the inventor's brother who was associated with him in his clockworks in Plymouth. This model is in the James Arthur Collection of New York University. (HC)

ELI WHITNEY, readily identified as the inventor of the cotton gin by any schoolchild, was more important in Connecticut as a pioneer in the manufacture of firearms made of machined interchangeable parts. Whitney founded a factory near East Rock in Hamden in 1798 for the manufacture of rifles. This portrait of him was painted in 1822 by Samuel F. B. Morse. Both inventors were graduates of Yale College.

THIS FIRST NEWSPAPER ADVERTISEMENT for the Aetna Insurance Company appeared in the *Connecticut Courant* of July 26, 1819. The company then had its offices at Morgan's Exchange Coffee House.

THE ASYLUM FOR THE DEAF AND DUMB, built in 1821, housed the American School for the Deaf until it was torn down in 1919 to make way for the present building of the Hartford Fire Insurance Company. The asylum was opened in 1817 under the direction of Thomas H. Gallaudet, who had been sent to Europe to study techniques of teaching the deaf. One of the first pupils of the school was Alice Cogswell, the deaf child of Dr. Mason F. Cogswell, who had fought for the school after Alice became totally deaf from spotted fever. A statue of Gallaudet and little Alice now stands on the grounds of the school in West Hartford. The original asylum gave its name to one of Hartford's main thoroughfares, Asylum Avenue. (HC)

[ 36 ]

THE FARMINGTON AQUEDUCT, part of the ambitious Farmington Canal system, opened to limited traffic in late 1828. A wooden trough supported by native stone piers carried boats plying the canal from New Haven to Northhampton, Massachusetts, over the Farmington River. Financial difficulties and competition from railroads ended the canal's operation in 1847; but its few years of operation stimulated the growth of New Haven.

AN EARLY VIEW OF Hartford from the Connecticut River around 1835: The old State House by Bullfinch is the domed building at right center. (HC)

ONE OF THE MORE SPECTACULAR FIRES in early Hartford is shown in this lithograph by J. G. Kellogg. In the early morning hours of August 5, 1839, a large building located on State House Square between the Hartford and Exchange banks caught fire and sustained heavy damage, The lithograph provides a view of early fire-fighting equipment and methods, and also shows what Hartford's State Street looked like in 1839.

[ 37 ]

THE MAIN STREET Stone Bridge over Hartford's Park River, was built in 1833. At that time, it was the largest stone arch in the state. The bridge still stands, but a highway passes under it now. The river is underground. (HC)

LAUNCHED in New Bedford, Massachusetts, in 1842, the *Charles W. Morgan* was America's last wooden whaling ship. Now on permanent exhibition at Mystic Seaport, this is how the old ship looked in 1940 before she was grounded in the sand at the seaport. She made thirty-seven whaling voyages, the longest of them lasting five years.

"THE SWEDISH NIGHTINGALE," Jenny Lind, was important in Connecticut history for two reasons. First she was promoted by the state's greatest impresario, Bridgeport's P. T. Barnum; second, she caused a near-riot in 1951 in Hartford when her concert at the Fourth Church was twice oversold. The singer had to jump out of the rear window to escape the overly enthusiastic crowd. Subsequently, this notice appeared: "We were informed by Jenny Lind's agent that she would give one or two concerts here on her return from the West, but after the treatment she has received, we can hardly expect to see her again." (HC)

THE HARTFORD PUBLIC HIGH SCHOOL, established in 1638, is the oldest educational institution in the state and one of the oldest in the country. This brick building at Asylum and Ann streets was occupied by the high school in 1847, when the school began to admit girls as well as boys, and served as the high school building until 1870, when a new high school on Hopkins Street was built. (HC)

DOCTOR HORACE WELLS was the guinea pig for his own invention, laughing gas (nitrous oxide), on December 11, 1844. This drawing shows Dr. John M. Riggs with the pulled tooth of Dr. Wells in the Hartford offices of the inventor of the anesthetic. (HC)

WHALE OIL ROW in New London as it looks today: The four houses are believed to be one of the only existing rows of American Greek Revival structures. They were built in 1830, during an era which saw New London rise to the third most-important whaling port in America. (HC)

HARTFORD'S HALL OF RECORDS was housed in this elegant brownstone building with a mansard roof at the corner of Pearl and Trumbull streets from 1853 until the present municipal building was opened in 1915. Before it was razed in 1940, it served as draft headquarters during World War I, as a service club for veterans afterward, and as an office building. (HC)

THE SECOND FLOOR OF the center building on Hartford's Main Street housed the Phoenix Insurance Company in 1854. The rent was $400 a year. (HC)

RAILROADING began to replace other forms of transportation in the 1840s when the old Hartford Railroad Station of the New York, New Haven and Hartford was built. This old lithograph shows what the predecessor of Hartford's present Union Station, built in 1849, looked like in the years before the Civil War. (HC)

THE GIANT CHARTER OAK that stood in front of Samuel Wyllys' house in Hartford became famous because Connecticut's original charter was once hidden there so that English governor Edmund Andros could not seize it in 1687 when he attempted to reorganize the New England states and New York into a royal dominion. When the great tree, which the Indians revered before the coming of the white man, crashed down on the morning of August 21, 1856, tiny pieces of furniture and other mementos were carved from the wood, some of which are exhibited at the Connecticut State Library. (HC)

SHETUCKET STREET in Norwich before the Civil War.

NEW HAVEN'S LONG WHARF about 1860: The Elm City Flouring Mill shared the docks with E. Pendleton, Ship Chandler and Provisions, and Hotchkiss & Sons' coal business. (NHR)

SAMUEL COLT, who was born in Hartford in 1814, carved a model of the Colt revolver while on his first sea voyage on which he embarked at the age of sixteen. Upon his return, he produced working models of a pistol and rifle using revolving cylinders and percussion firing. He received a patent in 1836, and by the 1850s was advertising the US Dragoon, the US Navy pistol, and Wells Fargo percussion cap Colt revolvers; the engravings on the ad show *(facing page)* the decorations on the cylinders for the three models. His original office building *(below)* was demolished in the 1940s to make way for modern industrial buildings at the present Colt complex.

[ 46 ]

THE YALE CAMPUS in 1860, just before the Civil War: In the foreground, rounding Chapel and College streets, is the fence defining the boundary between town and gown, which was moved within the quadrangle in 1888, when Osborn Hall was built. In the background is the Old Brick Row, of which only Connecticut Hall now remains. It was the most unpopular hall when this photograph was taken and was described as "dilapidated, scabby and malodorous with the must of ages." The Old Brick Row was completed in the early 1800s, and most of its buildings had been razed by the beginning of the next century.

THE NATIONS' FIRST WOMAN DENTIST, Emeline Roberts Jones of New Haven and Danielson, travelled in the years before the Civil War from town to town in eastern Connecticut and Rhode Island, using this portable dentist's chair. Mrs. Jones, pictured behind the chair, had learned to drill and fill from her husband. The chair and portrait are in the Thomas W. Evans Museum and Dental Institute of the School of Dentistry of the University of Pennsylvania. (HC)

**GLASTONBURY'S GIDEON WELLES** served as Secretary of the Navy under Lincoln and Johnson, reorganizing the department and revitalizing a sea force that had greatly deteriorated at the time of his takeover. He was instrumental in the building of the first ironclads. Before his political career he had been involved with a number of newspapers, among them the *Hartford Times* and the *Hartford Evening Press*. Welles sits here at the right of President Lincoln.

**A NEW MUNICIPAL WATER SYSTEM** for New Britain brought out a crowd to watch the first gush from Central Fountain in 1860. The First Congregational Church of New Britain (its steeple cut off by the original photographer) is at left. The Soldiers Monument now stands where the old fountain once stood. (HC)

THE "GRAND TORCHLIGHT PROcession" of the "Wide-Awakes" marched through Hartford on July 27, 1860, in support of Lincoln and his vice-presidential running-mate Hannibal Hamlin of Maine. Formed in Hartford, the Wide-Awakes gave protection to Republican candidates trhoughout the 1860s. The engraving appeared in the *New York Illustrated News*.

MAIN STREET IN HARTFORD is seen from two vantage points five years apart: The 1860 photo, taken from Talcott Street *(facing page, bottom)*, shows the dark tower of Christ Church Cathedral in the right foreground; little else remains. The other photograph *(below)*, taken in 1865 from Asylum Street, has a horsedrawn jitney in the street. Again, about the only survivor except for buildings in the distance, is a church—in this case, the First Church of Christ (Center Church), seen at center with the ornate triple-decked spire. (HC)

[ 49 ]

THIS WAS THE AFTERMATH of an attack on a pro-South newspaper in Bridgeport on August 24, 1861. The *Weekly Farmer,* a peace paper, had applauded the Union defeat at Bull Run and defended the rebels, claiming they were only fighting for their rights. A mob, led by returned three-month-soldiers, broke into the *Farmer's* offices, threw paper and light equipment out of the windows, and smashed the presses beyond repair. The photograph, never before reproduced in a book, shows what downtown Bridgeport looked like at the time of the Civil War. (BPL)

[ 50 ]

THE NEW HAVEN GREEN, or Public Square, in the 1860s: The first municipal transportation system with its horse-drawn trolleys was established in 1861. On the green are Trinity Episcopal Church at left, the New Haven State House, Center Congregational Church, and United Church, with Yale College in the background. (NHR)

HARTFORD'S BUSHNELL PARK at the time of the Civil War, seen from Wells Street near Main, shows Trinity College in the upper left-hand corner, on the present site of the State Capitol. Trinity, originally named Washington College when it was founded in 1823, later moved south to its present campus. About the same time, these balloon ascensions were photographed in Bushnell Park. Both pictures show the Park River in the foreground; the river was buried after flooding in the 1930s. (HC)

THE COSTLIEST FIRE in nineteenth-century Hartford was the $2 million Colt's Armory disaster on February 5, 1864, which destroyed the Portland-stone building only ten years after its completion. One man died in the fire and more than 1,700 workers were safely evacuated. Less than forty-five minutes after the fire was discovered, the gilded dome topped by a colt pawing the air collapsed. These two photographs were taken after the fire had died away and show the ruins of the three-story, 500-foot-long factory building. The brick building was rebuilt afterwards.

# New Citizens, New Cities

THE FIFTY YEARS between the end of the Civil War and the end of the Great War brought thousands upon thousands of new citizens crowding into Connecticut's cities. With them, Connecticut began to change from a small rural state of Yankee traders and farmers into a more pluralistic place where men whose English was broken into a score of accents built new businesses and buildings. As the new people came, the old ones began to move to the outskirts, building new frame houses or brick mansions along the shaded boulevards leading to the country.

From 1850 to 1870, the cities experienced great growth and the whole population in the state changed in character. By 1870, 21 per cent of the residents of Connecticut were foreign-born. The leading ethnic group was the Irish, who made up two units in the Civil War, and by 1870 comprised 13 per cent of the state's population and 20 per cent of the population of its largest city, New Haven. In the twenty years from mid-century to 1870, New Haven had grown from 20,345 to 50,840; in the same period, Hartford rose from 13,555 to 37,743, while Bridgeport, then becoming the third city in the state jumped from 7,560 to 19,835. Between 1850 and 1870, the population of the state went from 370,792 to 537,454—an increase of 45 per cent.

So the cities began to spread outward, with the men of wealth and position building their estates on the avenues which radiated out from the centers of the cities. In the 1850s, before his death in 1863, Samuel Colt had built his "Armsmear" on Hartford's Wethersfield Avenue, but it was still close to his factories in the center of the city. In Bridgeport, P. T. Barnum built a series of Xanadus before the Civil War and after: Iranistan in 1848, Lindencroft in the late 1850s, and Waldemere ("Woods-by-the-Sea") in 1868-69. Mark Twain built his new house, shaped like a riverboat, on Hartford's Farmington Avenue in 1874. And these were but the most famous and spectacular of the huge dark Victorian palaces which went up along the narrow dirt thoroughfares that reached out from the cities under arches of overhanging elms.

Railroads superseded shipping as the most common means of moving goods and raw materials between cities and states, and also began to cut into the passenger business done by the steamships that plied Connecticut's rivers and Long Island Sound. By the late 1860s, the New York and New Haven Railroad was one of New England's most prosperous businesses. In the cities, horse-drawn trolleys began to appear, and the world's first commercial telephone service began in New Haven in 1878.

The 1870s saw the end of the system of having two capitals, set up under the 1818 Constitution. Hartford outbid the more populous New Haven for the honor, and Richard Marshall Upjohn was hired to design the new Capitol which opened for legislative business in 1879 on land bought from Trinity College overlooking Bushnell Park. Built at a cost of $2,533,524.43, the new state Capitol, which has been described as "the world's most beautiful ugly building," was constructed of marble and granite in a riot of architectural styles, topped by a twelve-sided gilded dome.

Early labor legislation was among the first business transacted in the Capitol's first session. In 1886, the Assembly enacted a law stating that "no child under 13 years of age shall be employed in any mechanical, mercantile or manufacturing establishment." In 1887, maximum hours of labor were set at 10 hours a day, and 60 hours weekly for women and minors. The Knights of Labor, founded in 1869, had 37 members in the legislature in 1885-86; it was supplanted by the Connecticut Federation of Labor, founded in 1887, which helped to foster passage of a series of labor laws during the years between 1888 and 1903.

The 1890s in Connecticut were marked by a political deadlock which extended the governorship of Morgan G. Bulkeley of Hartford, because of a fight between the Republican-dominated House of Representatives and the Democrat-controlled Senate over whether the 1890 election was legal. On January 19, 1891, Governor Bulkeley announced that he would remain in office until the trouble was resolved, and a year later the state Supreme Court ruled in his favor. During this period, the state ran out of money, but Bulkeley arranged with the Aetna Life Insurance Company, which he headed, to pay the bills.

The turn of the century saw the beginnings of the heaviest immigration into Connecticut. By 1910, 30 percent of the state's 1,114,756 citizens were foreign-born, and the influx of new people again expanded the populations of the cities. Both New Haven and

ACTOR EDWIN BOOTH, brother of Lincoln's assassin John Wilkes Booth, was still a big box-office attraction in 1869. He broke all box-office records at Roberts' Opera House on Main Street, Hartford, with his performance as Hamlet that year. The take for the two-night stand? $3,011. (HC)

THIS ENGRAVING of a Bridgeport munitions factory gives a picture of manufacturing in the latter half of the nineteenth century. In an effort to speed production to meet the demands of of warring European nations, hand work had been eliminated, and cartridges were shaped, loaded, tested, and counted by machine. (HC)

Bridgeport passed the 100,000 mark in the early years of the century, and in 1910, nearly 90 per cent of the population lived in cities.

The years before World War I also gave rise to new industries in the cities. Col. A. A. Pope of Hartford, who had been making Columbia bicycles since 1878, built and marketed the high-priced Columbia Electric Phaeton in 1907; the company later switched to gas-driven cars before the automobile industry died out in Hartford. Booming Bridgeport began building the Locomobile in 1902, with an all-steel frame-sliding gear transmission, and vertical cylinder motor. The company made cars until 1929.

When American went to war in 1917, Connecticut's armaments industry again provided much of its firepower. Munitions poured out of the "Big Five:" Remington Arms and Ammunition and Remington Union Metallic in Bridgeport; Winchester Repeating Arms and Marlin-Rockwell in New Haven; and Colt's Patent Firearms in Hartford. John M. Browning of Colt's developed the heavy Browning water-cooled machine gun, the light Browning automatic rifle, and the Browning synchronized aircraft gun. Guns were not the state's only contribution to the war effort, however; about eighty percent of the state's industries were put to work turning out supplies for the Army and Navy.

As for fighting men, Connecticut sent approximately 67,000. The most important unit was the 102nd Infantry of New England's Yankee Division, the Twenty Sixth. Field artillery, cavalry, signal corps, ambulance and field hospital units also went into the Twenty Sixth. Connecticut units saw heavy action at Seicheprey, Chateau-Thierry, Aisne-Marne, Epieds, Trugny, Vigneuiles, and Verdun. The 102nd Infantry sustained more than 4,100 casualties in the War.

THIS AERIAL VIEW OF HARTFORD was drawn in the late 1860s, looking east toward the Connecticut River and East Hartford in the distance. In the foreground, on the banks of the Park River, was the Sharps Rifle Manufacturing Company, which had turned out Union rifles during the Civil War.

Near the left-hand side of the picture, looking like a cut-off pyramid, was the source of Hartford's water supply, the Lord's Hill Reservoir. The railroad tracks all converge in the center of the drawing on the old Union Station, the white building with twin towers in front.

THE SECOND HOME OFFICE of the Travelers Insurance Companies was in the first floor and basement of the Railroad Block on Asylum Street in Hartford, where it operated from 1865 to 1872. The company was founded by James Goodwin Batterson, whose first policy was for two cents—to insure an acquaintance for $1,000 while he walked home for lunch. To the left of the Travelers' home office (the building in the center), is the old Union Station. In the foreground is the Park River as it winds through Bushnell Park.

THE FIRST COMPANY, Governor's Foot Guard, lined up on Hartford's Central Row to honor Pres. U. S. Grant on July 2, 1870. The dome of the old State House rises behind the trees. (HC)

THE PRINTERY of Case, Lockwood and Brainard stood abandoned on Trumbull Street in Hartford about 1870, as the company had moved into a new plant in 1867. Originally the old county jail, built in 1794, the building then served as a lodging house "for a swarm of black and white families" from 1836 to 1838, when it became the second home of the printing and book bindery which is now known as Connecticut Printers.

BUBSER'S on Mulberry Street in Hartford (a street which is no more) was a popular spot in the 1870s. Bubser's sold beer, wine, and liquors at retail and wholesale, and had a hall for hire.

THE UNITED STATES HOTEL on State Street was one of the finest hotels of the latter half of the nineteenth century in Hartford. The Honiss Oyster House, the city's oldest restaurant still doing business, opened in the basement of the hotel in 1845. The hotel was demolished in the 1920s, and the Honiss moved for a while, but it continues where it began more than one hundred and thirty years ago. (HC)

MARK TWAIN had a series of twelve stereopticon slides taken at his house in Hartford around 1875, four years after he came to the city. The exterior *(above)* shows the present Mark Twain Memorial when it was new, before the trees grew, and before the kitchen wing was added in 1881. Farmington Avenue was a dirt road then, lined with fences. The photograph below shows Mark Twain and Mrs. Clemens with Dr. and Mrs. Jackson. Dr. Jackson was immortalized in *Innocents Abroad,* Twain's first book published in Hartford, by the American Publishing Company. During his two decades in Hartford, Twain also wrote *The Adventures of Tom Sawyer, The Adventures of Huckleberry Finn, Life on the Mississippi,* and *A Connecticut Yankee in King Arthur's Court.* (HC)

DOWNTOWN NEW HAVEN shortly after the Civil War: This is Church Street in 1872, showing the Tontine Hotel, brick residences, and the old Third Congregation Church. The New Haven Green is in the foreground.

THE YALE GLEE CLUB, shown here in 1865, was founded in 1861. (HC)

COLLEGE STREET in New Haven in the 1870s after completion of Yale University's Farnam Hall on the site of the second president's house.

THESE IDEALIZED VIEWS of South Norwalk (top) and Southport harbor (bottom) appeared in a magazine in the 1870s.

STEAMBOATS plied the state's major rivers and the Long Island Sound from the early 1880s. The *Capitol City,* docked at Hartford at the foot of State Street, was one of the principal river boats of the latter half of the nineteenth century and was the last steamboat on the Connecticut River in 1931, when service ended. The *Rosedale,* owned by the Bridgeport Steamboat Company, ran between Bridgeport and New York.

TEAMS OF OXEN were used in the middle nineteenth century to open this wooden drawbridge over the Mystic River *(below).* The oxen pulled back the bridge on fixed rollers onto the road on the east river bank, enabling vessels to pass through. This photograph of the Mystic, taken in 1865 or 1866, shows the Exchange Building or Washington Hall, built in 1850, but destroyed by fire in 1885. (Mystic Seaport)

AS RAIL TRAVEL BECAME the accepted mode of transportation between Connecticut cities in the latter half of the nineteenth century, train wrecks became more common. One of the worst in the state's history was the "Moody and Sankey" wreck of 1878, so called because the train of the Connecticut Western line was returning from a revival meeting in Hartford led by the evangelists Moody and Sankey when it plunged through the west span of a bridge over the Farmington River near Tariffville. Thirteen persons died and seventy were injured. The passengers were singing spirituals, among them "Yes, We'll Gather at the River" when the train fell into the icy waters of the Farmington. The relief train sent out from Hartford was Engine No. 9, the "Simsbury," shown below.

HORSE TROLLEYS still crowded New Haven streets in 1880. The street banner over Chapel Street (looking west from State Street, towards the New Haven Green) announces the Yale-Princeton game to be played on June 9. At the time, the Southern New England Telephone Company was located in the Yale National Bank Safe Deposit Vault building at right. (NHR)

THE COLLEGE PUMP served as a gathering place on the Yale Campus in the late nineteenth century. The pump was located beside the Old Laboratory, the fourth building constructed at Yale, which stood from 1872 to 1888. The building served successively as a dining hall and kitchen, as Benjamin Silliman's laboratory, and as the first home of the Yale Co-op. For the work that Silliman did within its white-washed brick walls, it became known as "one of the most important centers of chemical science in America."

DIGNIFIED APPROACHES to both engineering and football typify Yale of the 1880s. In 1883, Prof. William A. Norton, third from the left in a high silk hat, supervised the work of his last class of engineering students. His appointment to the Yale faculty in 1852 had marked the start of formal instruction in engineering. His class here is equipped with suits and bowlers for a field exercise in surveying. An 1888 photo *(below)* shows the "iron-men" team of that year when Yale held all of its thirteen opponents scoreless. Among the stalwarts on the team were the celebrated Amos Alonzo Stagg, left, and Pudge Hefflfinger, back row, center. (HC)

THE CELEBRATED ARCHITECT Ithiel Town designed this Greek Revival State House in New Haven which stood on the New Haven Green between the Trinity Episcopal Church and the Center Congregational Church. Construction was begun in 1827 and completed in 1831, and the General Assembly met in alternate years in the New Haven State House until 1874. This photograph was taken as demolition of the structure began in 1889. (HC)

[ 66 ]

THE FIRST HOME of the Bridgeport Public Library was the Burroughs Building on Main and John streets, built in 1872. Groceries and men's and boys' clothing were sold on the ground floor in 1883; the library was on the second floor. (BPL)

BANJO AND CAMERA were the main props for this outing at Saybrook's Fenwick Grove around 1885. Attire was hardly what one might call casual, and the whole business seems serious.

THE BUSINESS in this block of Main Street, Middletown, in 1888 included E. B. Smith, stoves and plumbing; Chaffee & Shaw, fine ales, cigars and tobacco; and C. R. Newell, meat. Charles R. Newell is at right and his sons, Isaac and Walter, are in the foreground.

THIS VIEW of Hartford's Old Fish Market, taken around 1880, shows how the waterfront looked at that time, and the West India storehouses of Chapin and Burr at Ferry and Commerce streets. (HC)

HARTFORD PUBLIC HIGH SCHOOL, razed in the 1960s to make way for an interstate highway, looked like this in 1883.

A PANORAMIC VIEW of Hartford from high up in the new State Capitol in 1880: At lower left, the Memorial Arch, dedicated to fallen Civil War soldiers, is under construction. The Park River winds through Bushnell Park, and a fountain plays at right in one of the park's ponds. (HC)

[ 68 ]

GENERATIONS OF IMMIGRANTS and their children learned the three R's at Hartford's Brown School at Market and Talcott streets on the old East Side. Built in 1866, the school stood at the site until 1945. This photograph was taken in the late 1800s.

HARTFORD'S OLD COUNTY BUILDING at Trumbull and Allyn streets was completed in 1885 and housed the functions of county government until the current Superior Court building on Washington Street was completed. It was demolished in 1930.

*THE BLACK CROOK,* said to be America's first musical comedy, was among the attractions at Roberts' Opera House in Hartford during the 1880s. After running sixteen months in New York, this Faustian musical melodrama toured the United States for more than forty years. (HC)

LATE SUNDAY NIGHT on March 11, 1888, a light snow began to fall. It stopped about midnight Monday, but started up again and didn't start to tail off until Tuesday afternoon. Hartford ended up with thirty-six inches of snow. Elsewhere in the state, accumulations went up to fifty inches. When the snow stopped, horses and walkers struggled through the streets and sidewalks of Hartford's Main Street. Bridgeport's State Street is shown partly dug out, with piles of snow towering over the little girl in the foreground. (HC-BPL)

PHARMACISTS wore suits and aprons in 1888, when this photograph was taken at Hartford's old Exchange Corner. The store's windows, awnings, and signs advertise mineral water, soda, Poland water, drugs, medicines, trusses, elastic stockings, and supporters. The "homeopath pharmacy" was open all night. Exchange Corner was on Main Street around the corner from State Street. (HC)

[ 70 ]

THE ASCENSION DAY PARADE of the Knights Templars about 1887 provides a fine view of Hartford's Main Street with its horse-drawn trolleys, bicycles, and hansom cabs.

A GATLING GUN was mounted on this police wagon, shown in front of the Hartford Police Department at 38 Kinsley Street in the 1890s. Police Chief George F. Bill is barely visible in the window behind the horses' heads.

THE FIRST RUBBER-TIRED CARRIAGE in Hartford, owned by T. A. Honiss, stopped in front of the State Capitol in 1893.

"OLD JUMBO" *(right)* joined the Hartford Fire Department in 1889 and stayed in service until 1929 when it was placed in reserve. James Swan, president of the Swan Manufacturing Company in Seymour, bought it in 1932, and later turned it over to the collection of antique automobiles at the Melton Museum in Norwalk. Here Swan is shown driving "Old Jumbo" to the museum in 1959.

THE TROLLEY CAR became the chief means of mass transit in the late 1880s; this is Hartford's first trolley car, No. 50, of the Hartford and Wethersfield Horse Railroad Company, which carried passengers along the route from Hartford to Wethersfield on Main Street and Wethersfield Avenue beginning in 1880. This photograph, owned by Elmer E. White of Binghamton, New York, shows what the countryside to the south of downtown Hartford looked like this in the 1880s. (HC)

HARTFORD FIELDED this "polo team" in 1888. Apparently the game was a kind of roller skate hockey.

A BOILER EXPLOSION killed twenty-two occupants of the Park Central Hotel in Hartford on February 18, 1899. The blast left the fifteen-year-old hotel a shambles of brick, plaster, and woodlath, and three hundred persons—including four companies of National Guardsmen—toiled through the ruins in search of survivors, some of whom were pinned in the debris as long as eight hours. The five-story building stood at 54 High Street, a block from the railroad station.

BICYCLING was the rage of the Gay Nineties. The Hartford Cycle Club *(above)*, in caps and bowlers, rounded the corner of Main Street onto Central Row on high wheelers in 1890. To prove that cycling wasn't for men only, the Ladies Cycle Club of Hartford *(left)*, posed in front of the Memorial Arch later that same year. Other bicyclists of the 1890s were champion racer A. W. "Lonnie" Warren *(below right)* on his chain-driven two-wheeler, and Harry R. Hayden of East Hartford *(below left)*, with his high-wheeler. (HC)

TWO VIEWS OF WATERBURY around 1890, shown in an engraving from a contemporary magazine: Among the products of the factory city listed in that periodical were pins, needles, hosiery, machinery, webbing, lamps, knick-knacks, beer, paper boxes, malleable iron, silverware, electric goods of all kinds, carriages, aluminum, blank-books, and Waterbury watches. But for nearly a century, the most important product of Waterbury had been its brass. The first successful American castings of brass bars were performed in Waterbury between 1806 and 1809. The city's most important manufacturer, Scovill Manufacturing Company, was founded in 1850.

HORSE-DRAWN VEHICLES shared the streets with trolleys on Hartford's Asylum Street in 1890. Some of the buildings on the left side of the street still stand, but the right-hand side has been rebuilt at least twice since the 1890s.

THE WEST SIDE of Bridgeport's Main Street between Bank and John streets looked like this around 1890. There were gaslights, hansom carriages, and a clutter of signs advertising baked goods, hanging lamps, custom tailoring, boots and shoes, trunks and bags, and house-furnishing goods. (BPL)

THE CITY HOTEL, built in 1819, was Hartford's most important hostelry in the nineteenth century where a reception was held for the Marquis de Lafayette in 1824; where Charles Dickens celebrated his thirtieth birthday in 1842; Jefferson Davis, then U. S. Secretary of War, was a guest in 1853. It stood on Main Street, at the corner of Gold across from the Wadsworth Atheneum, until it was torn down in 1913, and the Palace Building, since razed, was built in its place. This photograph was taken in the 1890s, a few years before the building was remodeled into an office building. (HC)

COLUMBUS DAY 1892 brought out crowds on Main Street in downtown Bridgeport to watch a parade that included this float from the Concordia Society. Policemen in grey hats hold back the crowds of men in derbies and boaters and of women under parasols. (BPL)

THE WINTER of 1893 was so cold that the Bridgeport Harbor froze over. People crossed the ice to the lighthouse to pose for this photograph by Montignani. (BPL)

THE WINCHESTER Repeating Arms Company in New Haven had moved in the late nineteenth century to Munson and Canal (now Winchester Avenue) streets. By the turn of the century, Winchester, founded in 1866, employed more than 2,600 workers, and its brass mill was turning out more than four million pounds of metal. Its famous Winchester 73 had this testimony from Col. W. F. (Buffalo Bill) Cody: "I pronounce your improved Winchester the boss." Teddy Roosevelt said in 1875: "The Winchester is the best gun for any game to be found in the United States."

BOTH MAJOR CITIES on the Thames River, New London and Norwich, are shown in this engraving of the late nineteenth century. Norwich, at the top, was described as a city of "a very romantic aspect," with "noble avenues, with fine trees, antique and modern mansions, and very handsome public buildings." New London, below, is shown in a night view. Flanking the top view of Norwich are monuments to the Indian Sachem Uncas, right, and the Groton Monument commemorating those who were slain in the fight for Fort Griswold during the Revolution.

SMALL BOYS RACE with horse-drawn fire engines to get to the fire first on New Haven's Artizan Street in the 1890s. Workers of Herrick & Cowell, Machinists, are drawn to the front door by the firebells and racing hoofbeats. (NHR)

ONE OF THE PLEASURE SPOTS on Bridgeport's waterfront in the 1890s was the Black Rock Yacht Club. During the American Revolution, Black Rock had been the site of a fort to protect Penfield Mills and the bakehouse at Ash Creek. (BPL)

THE CONNECTICUT RIVER overflowed its banks in April 1895, and this is how it looked from the vantage point of the Aetna building. The far bank is East Hartford; part of Hartford had become an island.

THE FLAMBOYANT PERSONALITY of P. T. Barnum *(left)*, its most famous resident, dominated Bridgeport in the late 1900s. A promoter and hoaxer to the rest of the world, he was a political leader and philanthropist at home. Bridgeport also gave the world General Tom Thumb *(below)*, born in 1838 as Charles S. Stratton and rechristened by Barnum. Tom, 31 inches high at the age of twenty-five, married Lavinia Warren in 1863, and toured with her taking along special costumes, couches, and furniture until his death in 1883. Some of the appurtenances of Tom and Barnum can be seen in the Barnum Museum, built by the master showman himself as the Barnum Institute of Science and History. This 1893 view of the institute *(above)* was taken shortly after the building opened in 1893, two years after Barnum's death. It was envisioned as an exhibition hall for inventors and scientists and the Wright brothers exhibited their plane there. (Barnum Museum-BPL)

BARNUM brought out his circus elephants to test the strength of the new Stratford Avenue Bridge in Bridgeport, completed in 1888. The great showman himself is somewhere in the middle of the picture. (BPL)

A SPECTACULAR WRECK on the Central Vermont Tailroad in the Eagleville section of Mansfield in December 1896 was caused by the engine blowing up.

BACK IN THE DAYS before Hartford was cut off from its waterfront by dikes and highways, the Hartford Yacht Club operated out of this clubhouse built in 1895.

THE HARTFORD ORPHAN ASYLUM on Russ Street (seen here in 1897) was built in the late 1880s. In June 1888, it housed thirty-six girls and forty-eight boys. The orphanage has since been demolished.

ASYLUM AVENUE was one of Hartford's finest residential streets around the turn of the century, remaining beautiful well into the 1950s with trees that had been young in the 1890s hanging over the street. Today, little remains of the residential character of the street, but a few of the big old brick and brownstone mansions still stand, a few restored, others run down. The Asylum Hill Congregational Church, in the foreground, built of Portland stone in the Civil War era, remains today. (HC)

HOSIERY, GLOVES, laces, and "silk's warranted" were advertised on the awnings of the dry goods store of Sage, Allen & Company in 1896. The store is now one of Hartford's largest department stores with branches throughout the state. When the photograph above was taken, the major department store was Brown, Thomson & Company *(below)*, with a building designed by Henry Hobson Richardson. Its specialty was apparently cloaks. Sage-Allen was then located at Main and Pratt streets; it has since moved across the street; Brown-Thomson is no longer in business, and today the building at Main and Temple streets houses part of the city's largest department store, G. Fox & Company.

[ 83 ]

TWO TYPES OF TRANSPORTATION—rails and canals—are shown side by side in this 1898 photograph in Windsor Locks. The wood-burning locomotive above made a daily run by the C. H. Dexter Plant.

NEW HAVEN'S MARLIN FIRE ARMS sold its repeaters with this advertisement *(right)* during the nineties. "Consider—" says the ad, "if you can keep the wet out of your rifle, it will not rust nor freeze. Only Marlin Repeaters have Solid Tops, shedding water like a duck's back." The company gave this rifle *(below)* to the famous lady sharpshooter who was a star attraction with the Buffalo Bill Wild West Show in the late 1890s: Annie Oakley.

THE PRATT AND WHITNEY COMPANY, the forerunner of both an aircraft-engine builder in East Hartford and a maker of machine tools in West Hartford, made mailboxes in 1898 that were used in Hartford many years. The photograph of the factory on Capitol Avenue affords a view of what the interior of such a concern looked like around the turn of the century.

SAINT JOSEPH CATHEDRAL on an as-yet-unpaved Farmington Avenue in Hartford was consecrated on May 8, 1892, and served as the seat of the Hartford Diocese until it was destroyed by fire on the last day of 1956. The old Gothic church had marble and onyx altars, stained-glass windows, a gold-leaf rotunda, a $100,000 organ, and a ceiling inlaid with woods from every country in the world.

THE UNIVERSITY OF CONNECTICUT fielded this team with an interlocked line and a five-man backfield around 1900. At that time the school was still named the Storrs Agricultural College and was barely twenty years old, having been founded in 1881 in the town of Mansfield.

YALE ROWING TEAMS still competed in New Haven Harbor at the turn of the century when this photograph of the Yale Boat House was taken. Boathouses in the harbor were used from 1859 until 1934, when rowing had to be moved to the Housatonic River in Derby.

WASHINGTON STREET was one of turn-of-the-century Hartford's most beautiful thoroughfares with its huge, elegant mansions, its wrought iron fences, and its overhanging elm trees. (HC)

HARTFORD'S OLD EAST SIDE, where Constitution Plaza now stands as the city's first major redevelopment effort, looked like this near the end of the century. It was a section of Jewish and Italian immigrants at that time and in the years to come. This photograph was taken by P. P. Kimball at Temple and Market streets, looking north on Market. (HC)

HARTFORD'S CITY HALL now stands where these two wood frame buildings stood on Main Street at the turn of the century. To the left is the Wadsworth Atheneum, the city's art museum. A poster on the gambrel-roofed structure at left center advertises the coming of the Buffalo Bill Wild West Show. (HC)

[ 88 ]

A BARBER SHOP, a bakery, a flower shop, and a newsboy were among the businesses operating in Bridgeport's Arcade in 1899. (BPL)

TWO PHOTOGRAPHS of Hartford's Main Street made five years apart give an idea of what it was like to walk through downtown in 1895 and 1900. The street was paved by that time, and trolley tracks ran down its center. The top photo, with the steeple of Center Congregational Church on the left and City Hotel below it in the foreground, provides a view that reaches to State Street and the Brown-Thomson store, with its pointed tower. In the photo below, the corner of State Street is in the right foreground. Both photographs are looking north.

[ 89 ]

THE BOROUGH OF BRIDGEPORT, first in Connecticut, celebrated its centennial in 1900, and City Hall was decked out for the occasion. At this point, Bridgeport was recognized as one of the great industrial cities of the new world; ammunitions, the first gramophones, sewing machines, and rust-proof corsets were only a few of the products that came pouring out of the borough. (BPL)

NICOLA MARCANTONIO, left, and his half-brother, Michael Luciano, were photographed in Hartford in 1900 shortly after they were reunited. They had come over from Potenza in Italy years apart, and Luciano had searched all over New England for his half-brother before finding him in Hartford.

THE CHOIR of New Haven's Church of the Redeemer on Whitney Avenue was photographed outside the church at the beginning of the new century.

THE OFFICES of the United Illuminating Company in New Haven looked like this shortly after the turn of the century. (NHR)

CONNECTICUT'S SUBMARINE INDUSTRY actually began in New Jersey in 1900 with the construction of the *Holland,* a $15,000 job for the U.S. Navy. John P. Holland, the inventor, emerges from the hatch of the ship at left. A shakedown cruise was made in 1900 *(below).* Though the ship wasn't built in Connecticut, it ended its life here, rusting away in a New Haven barn before it was scrapped. The Electric Boat Company was founded by Holland in Groton in 1924 and delivered its first order to the navy, the USS *Cuttlefish,* in 1931. (HC)

TURN-OF-THE-CENTURY visitors to Hartford could avail themselves of the comforts of the Turkish Room of the Allyn House, which opened in 1857 at the corner of Asylum and Trumbull streets. (Abraham Lincoln was a guest there before he was elected president.) And for the visitor and local resident alike there was Otto Hennig's saloon on Temple Street, as it looked in 1905.

NEW BRITAIN'S CENTRAL PARK and Main Street: Behind the park are the Hotel Russwin and the Baptist Church. By the turn of the century, New Britain had grown to a population of 26,000; in 1850 it had had only about 3,000 residents.

AMATEUR FISHERMEN on Long Island Sound display one of their catches in the photograph at left, one of a group of studies of the Connecticut shoreline done around 1900 by Thomas Lyons of Weathersfield. Also by Lyons is the picture below, which shows professional fishermen aboard the *Thistle* on the Connecticut River.

CLAMMING was a popular, enjoyable activity as the expression on this rather rakish-looking old gentleman indicates. The young fellow *(below)* seems to be scanning tidal pools for shellfish while his boat, forgotten for a minute, bobs between the rocks. (HC)

[ 94 ]

BEACH PARTIES were dressed-up affairs around 1900 when James Lyon of Wethersfield took this group of three photographs. The top picture provides a close-up of the garb of the day and also emphasizes that being photographed was a solemn occasion—except for the young woman in the center whose pose appears very liberated in contrast to the rest of the group. The center photograph is more candid and the gentleman seems to be gathering mussels from the tidal pools amid the rocks while two well-dressed companions, or passersby, observe. The group in the bottom photograph, depicted basking on a typical rock formation along Long Island Sound, must have been instructed not to look at the camera.
(HC)

THE THREE CHURCHES on New Haven Green were already nearly a hundred years old as the 1900s began. Trinity Church (at left) was completed in 1815 after designs by the famed New Haven architect Ithiel Towne. In the center is Center Church, built between 1812 and 1814 from Towne designs suggested by Saint Martin-in-the-Fields in Trafalgar Square, London. The United Church (at right), dedicated in 1815, was designed by David Hoadley.

MOSELEY'S NEW HAVEN HOUSE stood at the corner of Chapel and College streets, as seen in this 1890s photograph before the Hotel Taft was built. The New Haven House, owned in the late nineteenth century by Yale, remained a popular resort of its alumni, after the university sold it.

OSBORN HALL, " that fantastic dream in stone perched like a squatting toad with open lip," was built in 1888 and served as one of Yale's major lecture halls until it was demolished in 1926. It was built to close off the Old Campus from the growing town, but deafening noises of horses on the cobblestones and trolley cars rounding the corner of College and Chapel streets made some lectures impossible to hear. Among those who contended with the noise was former President William Howard Taft, who lectured in Osborn on law.

SAVIN ROCK in West Haven was synonymous with summer outings for nearly two centuries, though it changed from a place for seaside hotels and restaurants catering to summer trade in 1771 to a place of hotdog stands, side shows, and games of chance before it was demolished in the early 1970s. Its height probably came around the turn of the century when many of these attractions were new: A. M. Hammer's Victorian ice cream parlor over the water *(top right),* built in 1895; the 1,227-seat theater *(right),* built in 1900; and Miller's Casino *(above).* The Connecticut Building at Colonial Park *(below)* was built for the Chicago World's Fair in 1892, but was brought back to West Haven by public-spirited state residents. With its electric fountain, beautiful hotels, and good restaurants, Savin Rock was a kaleidoscope of lights, people, and gaiety when the century was young,

NORWICH'S CITY HALL is now housed in the brick building with the clock tower, which was the Courthouse in 1907. Norwich retains much of its nineteenth century aura today, but some of the buildings in the turn-of-the-century view have been demolished.

GRIDLEY HOUSE CORNER in Bristol in the early 1900s.

BRIDGEPORT'S GOLDEN HILL HOTEL looked like this on a summer day in 1900, with flags flying in the gentle breezes and guests and proprietors out on the front veranda to take the air. The owner, George F. Carr, stands at left and his son George, Jr., strikes a jaunty pose on the steps. The Golden Hill stood on Harrison Street. (BPL)

TYPICAL of a small Connecticut town around 1900 is this view of Thompson, with its dusty narrow Main Street and white church steeple rising above the frame houses and summer trees.

WATERBURY'S EXCHANGE PLACE in the early part of the twentieth century, after the introduction of trolleys, was a large open space adjoining the green to the southeast. It was then described as "an exceedingly busy quarter, as many of the most important financial, commercial, and shopping houses of the city are located here."

THIS BIRDS-EYE VIEW, taken from the Arrigoni Building, shows the southern end of Middletown and the Connecticut River beyond in 1910. About the same time, the street scene below was taken, showing oxen pulling a hay wagon through the city.

THE OLD DEPOT of the New York, New Haven and Hartford Railroad was built in the 1870s, about twenty years after the city of Putnam in eastern Connecticut was incorporated from parts of Pomfret, Thompson, and Killingly, and named for Gen. Israel Putnam, the Revolutionary War hero. The view below shows Main Street downtown looking south, about 1900.

TEXTILE MILLS began to spring up throughout eastern Connecticut in the early 1800s and continued to grow for more than a century until after World War II, when many of the cotton and wool manufacturers moved south in search of cheaper labor. But at the beginning of the new century, large mills dominated the centers of many eastern Connecticut towns. Here are two glimpses of some of the mill towns around the turn of the century: the Quinebaug Mills in Danielson, which had succeeded the small cotton mill begun in 1820 by Comfort Tiffany; and the Nightingale Mills in Putnam.

FLOATS COVERED WITH FLAGS, bunting, and children, and horses festooned with garlands were highlights of Decoration Day 1907, on Harrison Street in New Haven's Westville section. Decoration Day, begun in 1868, later became Memorial Day.

THE DAM in Bridgeport's Beardsley Park broke on July 29, 1905, and shortly thereafter this woman was photographed in the breach. The dam at Bunnell's Pond had helped supply power to Bridgeport. (BPL)

MEATS were still delivered by horse and wagon in Middletown in 1906. A glimpse of a residential street in Middletown is seen in the background.

W. F. BISHOP'S funeral home on State Street boasted this funeral carriage around the turn of the century. (BPL)

THE HARTFORD BRIDGE (now the Bulkeley Bridge) was opened in 1908. It cost $3 million and took three years to build; in its time, it was considered unusual for the broadness of its boulevard, and it still carries an interstate highway today. It had a number of predecessors, going back to 1809, but the one that lasted the longest was a covered bridge that carried traffic from East Hartford to Hartford from 1818 until 1895, when it burned in a spectacular fire witnessed by 20,000 people. Its interior had a trolley track. After the wooden bridge burned, ferry service was revived for a time. An 1895 photograph shows one of the boats, with the piles for the old bridge in the background.

A PARLOUR of a New Haven house in 1906 was illuminated by gaslights and warmed by a cast-iron fireplace. A banjo and a spinet provided live music, and Beethoven's bust shared the mantlepiece with family photographs.

HARTFORD WAS A PIONEER in the automobile industry in 1895, but by 1914 it was all over. Before automobile manufacture died out in the city, however, cars like the Pope-Hartford touring car, shown in a 1908 photograph *(left)*, and the Columbia racing car *(below)* were produced. At the wheel of the Columbia was driver Eddie Bald, a one-time expert bicycle racer. The chain-driven, pipe-cooled car was tried out in 1906 at Charter Oak Park in West Hartford. Among those watching the trial run was Hiram Percy Maxim, who established the Motor Carriage Department of the Pope Manufacturing Company, and later developed the Maxim Silencer. (HC)

A RUNAWAY LOCOMOTIVE, No. 321, ran through the wall of the Hartford Round House on July 8, 1905. The round house stood on the present site of the State Armory in Hartford. (HC)

HARTFORD was building cars, but the city's fire department still relied on old-fashioned horse power in 1910 when this photograph was taken in front of Firehouse No. 6 on Huyshope Avenue.

FRANK H. HARRIMAN built this triplane in South Glastonbury in 1910.

*MERCEDES,* billed as the "Astounding Musical Enigma," was the current show, and Frederick V. Bowers in *The Song Review* was coming next in the early years of the century when Poli's Globe Theater on Bridgeport's Main Street played vaudeville. The hat store next door to the Globe advertised its wares at $1.50 and $2.00 and the haberdasher on the other side of the marquee offered suits and overcoats for $10, $12.50, and $15. (BPL)

WILLIAM GILLETTE'S most famous role was that of Sherlock Holmes, and this is how he looked in the part, probably around 1910. But Gillette was more than an actor; he was also a playwright, not only of the *Sherlock Holmes* which has now been very successfully revived by the Royal Shakespeare Company, both in London and New York, but also of other rediscovered plays. Born in 1855 in Hartford's Nook Farm Colony where both Mark Twain and Harriet Beecher Stowe had their homes, Gillette built himself a castle in East Haddam, high over the Connecticut River, after his successes as Holmes. The castle is now in a Connecticut state park.

SOPHIE TUCKER, the self-styled "last of the red-hot mamas," was born in Hartford. This photograph, taken about 1908, shows her as she was when Ziegfeld put her in his "follies." He later fired her because she had stolen the show and angered his other stars. (HC)

ITALIAN IMMIGRANTS Nicola Marcantonio from Potenza and his wife Rosa from Campobasso posed proudly with their daughter Mary in 1910 in a Manchester photographer's studio.

ICE CUT ON TROUT BROOK in West Hartford was carried into the ice house on the bank of the small river, to be distributed by Hartford's Trout Brook Ice Company. In the spring of 1906, Hartford's three ice companies divided the town and agreed to service only the customers in their own districts. City newspapers condemned this as a "monopoly" and ice prices rose from 50 to 150 per cent in the first two weeks. Merchants complained and charged that "babies and old people would suffer." The "ice trust" was busted by the saloon keepers, who formed their own ice company; some in the new concern wanted to make ice artificially, but this was condemned by the competition as socialism. So the new company obtained natural ice from Massachusetts.

THE OLDEST NEWSPAPER in continuous circulation in the United States, *The Hartford Courant,* founded in 1764, moved into this building on State Street in 1880, and remained there for seventy years until it moved into its present building on Broad Street. Horse-drawn vehicles still shared the streets with horseless carriages when this photograph was taken, probably around 1910. (HC)

HARTFORD'S PRESENT CITY HALL was built by halves, as this photograph taken by Charles W. Cooke in 1912, shows. The project was cut into two stages because the city didn't appropriate enough money at the start of the project to begin the whole thing. Work began in 1912 with a $300,000 appropriation, and another $1 million was later appropriated to finish the rear half. The building was dedicated on November 4, 1915. (HC)

[ 111 ]

IN THE SUMMER OF 1914, Hartford's Riverside Park provided shade and playgrounds for the children of immigrants living on the nearby old East Side. (HC)

CHILDREN PLAY in the outdoor gymnasium in Hartford's Pope Park in 1914. The eighty-nine-acre park was given to the city in 1895 by industrialist Col. Albert A. Pope.

A BIRD'S-EYE VIEW of Hartford in 1914, seen from the dome of the State Capitol: In the foreground, near the Memorial Arch, are the old YMCA buildings, opened in 1893, and only recently demolished. The downtown had become crowded with multi-story buildings, many of them now-departed manufacturing plants.

FEEDING THE GULLS at Ocean Beach Park in New London was a formal pastime around 1910. Ocean Beach later became the site of a city-owned beach and amusement park.

THESE VIEWS of Chalkers Beach in Old Saybrook and Middle Beach Avenue in Madison show what Connecticut's shorelines looked like in the years between 1910 and 1920.

THE LAST TWO seventeenth-century buildings in Hartford stood at the corner of Main Street and Charter Oak Avenue until 1914, when they were demolished. (HC)

[ 114 ]

PARK STREET near the intersection of Main Street in downtown Hartford looked almost like a country town in the summer of 1916.

THE TRIPLE-DECKER BANNER HEADLINES and sub-headlines tell the story as it was known at the time. But by the time further investigations were completed, it turned out that, in all, sixty-four persons had died while in the care of the convalescent home of Mrs. Amy Archer-Gilligan in Windsor. Mrs. Gilligan was later convicted in 1916 of poisoning five of them. Her conviction was overturned, but she spent the rest of her life, forty-three years, as a mental patient. This macabre story is said to have provided the basis for the celebrated American stage comedy, *Arsenic and Old Lace*, by Joseph O. Kesselring.

FORMER PRESIDENT William Howard Taft is shown attending the thirty-fifth reunion of the Yale class of 1878. The Yale Bowl is in the background. Taft was the only Yale graduate to become President, and he went back to Yale as Kent Professor of Constitutional Law when he retired from the Presidency in 1913, shortly before this photograph was taken. (HC)

THE LAST GOVERNOR of Connecticut to be driven to his inauguration in a horse-drawn carriage was Marcus H. Holcomb, a Republican from Southington, shown here on his way to the State Capitol in Hartford in 1915. Also in the carriage, closed because of rain on that day, was the out-going governor, Simeon E. Baldwin, a Democrat from New Haven. (HC)

THE AMBULANCE of the Animal Rescue League of Bridgeport carries away a patient about 1915. The photograph was taken on Park Avenue in front of the grocery store of Walter J. Hartnett. One wonders if the "Prime Meats" advertised on his awning included horse meat. (BPL)

MEN OF COMPANY M of the 102nd Regiment *(below)* smoke while drying their socks somewhere in France during World War I. One of the regiment's commanding officers, Col. John H. "Machine Gun" Parker *(right)*, a regular Army officer, was awarded two Distinguished Service Cross citations and the Croix de Guerre. The 102nd served in Europe from January to November 1918 and suffered 4,150 casualties, with 476 killed. It fought at Chemin des Dames, Toul, Seicheprey, Chateau-Thierry, St. Mihiel, Troyon, and at Verdun, where it sustained its heaviest casualities.

BOYS WORE NECKTIES and knickers, and girls wore big bows and long dresses in 1918 when the third-grade class at Hartford's Southwest School was photographed on the steps of the school. Small class sizes were unusual in a city school like this one. The teacher had thirty-eight students to keep in line and teach.

[ 118 ]

VETERANS IN UNIFORM marched in the Independence Day Parade on July 4, 1919, down Bridgeport's Main Street. This view, looking north from State Street, shows that dentists were free to advertise in those days. In the left center, the sign above the shingle for "Victrolas" says: "Why not let Dr. Fagan DENTISTS examine your teeth now . . . Haf-A-Minit . . . X-Ray Exams." (BPL)

# *The Modern Era - Less Steady Habits*

WHEN THE GREAT WAR ENDED, Connecticut was only 13 years away from its 300th birthday, and during its first 287 years, the colony-state had changed slowly, from an agrarian to an urban society. "The Land of Steady Habits" had truly deserved its name; it had been a generally conservative state, with progressive elements occasionally forcing needed changes.

But with the boom years of the twenties, with the proliferation of the car and the movie and the radio, with the coming of the flapper and the Babbitt, Connecticut began to change more rapidly.

First the car helped to build once rural areas into suburbs; from 1920 to 1930, while Hartford was growing by a healthy 19 percent, six of its suburbs were far outstripping it, increasing 65 percent in population. One of the suburbs, West Hartford, tripled in size during the decade—from 8,854 in 1920, to 24,941 in 1930. The automobile made other changes in the state too. By the 1930s, Connecticut began building a network of major new highways, and after World War II, the highway boom intensified; now multi-lane tunnels and bridges carved up old city neighborhoods.

Natural disasters also caused changes; floods in 1936 and 1938 caused the construction of river dikes that cut Hartford off from the river that had first made it important; parts of the Park River were put in conduits and more conduits were built after the 1955 floods.

World War II fostered the growth of what was to become the state's major industry: aviation. Aircraft accounted for more than $4 billion in war contracts, half of the $8-billion work done in the state during the war years. Pratt & Whitney Aircraft turned out more than 500,000 engines in East Hartford, and Hamilton Standard in Windsor Locks made 1,000,000 propellers. At Groton, Electric Boat built more than 75 submarines. To the present, both industries continue to dominate the state's economy. Connecticut also sent more than 210,000 men into the war, with about 5,700 fatalities.

MARSHAL FERDINAND FOCH, commander of the Allied Forces in World War I, visited Hartford on December 13, 1921. Here he leaves the Old State House between lines of the Governor's Foot Guard. To the marshal's right is Gov. Everett J. Lake. (HC)

When the war was over there was a sudden demand for housing, and a postwar building effort began to provide returning veterans with places to live. This also had a major impact on the cities and towns; public housing blocks and small houses on tiny lots remain as examples of hasty and unplanned construction that blights urban and suburban areas alike. Then, in the 1950s, the cities were dealt the heaviest blow of all. Redevelopment began as an idea of great promise, but too often it merely turned nineteenth-century neighborhoods of character into faceless, inhuman plazas and skyscrapers. The original Connecticut city of Hartford was the most badly damaged by redevelopment; it lost its old East Side where generations of immigrants had begun their Americanization, where open-air groceries, bakeries, and pizzerias had stood side by side with old churches and synagogues. The capital city also lost all its old vaudeville and movie houses, and became something of a ghost town after dark. New Haven lost much of its charm, too, but while redevelopment was taking down old theaters and a highway was slicing through old neighborhoods, an ambitious program of restoration was bringing back the beauties of places like Conte Square and Dwight Street. Some of the buildings which replaced the old, elegant brick and stone buildings in Hartford and New Haven had architectural character; many others did not. But smaller cities had worse problems; often old downtowns were razed only to be replaced by parking lots or vast, empty, windswept gardens for ragweed and rubbish.

There were also political changes during the years from 1918 onward. The twenties were the last years when the Republicans could be more or less confident of winning in the state and the cities; Connecticut's long-time GOP boss, J. Henry Roraback, got his candidates elected easily enough before the crash, and ran the politics in the state from his rooms at the old Allyn Hotel in Hartford. But in 1930, the Democratic nominee, Wilber L. Cross, was elected to the first of four terms. With the election of Raymond E. Baldwin (later to become both U.S. Senator and chief of the state Supreme Court) in 1938, the GOP moved back into the executive mansion, and until the mid-fifties, the party in the governor's office changed almost every election. But with the inauguration in 1955 of the state's first Jewish governor, Abraham Ribicoff, later a U.S. Senator, the Democrats under the leadership of the late John M. Bailey assumed almost unbroken control of the Capitol. They have been defeated in only one gubernatorial election since then.

THE LIBRARY CARAVAN of the Bridgeport Public Library visits Seaside Village, which had served as World War I housing, to sign up new members in 1922. The touring car which served as the Caravan is decorated with signs proclaiming, "A Book is Every Kiddies Friend . . . Take One Home Today" and "Buried Treasures in Public Libraries." (BPL)

YALE UNIVERSITY'S celebrated Harkness Tower was completed in 1921. The Gothic tower still looks much the same, although the stone building in the left foreground, the old Kent laboratory, has given way to a residential college, and Library Street, which ran between the lab and Harkness, has disappeared. Construction of Harkness and the Memorial Quadrangle was begun in 1917, but delayed because of interruptions during World War I.

NEW HAVEN'S University Street, now gone, looked like this in the 1920s before the construction of Jonathan Edwards residential college on the right.

THESE TWO SNAPSHOTS, taken in the twenties show New Haven's Hillhouse High School *(below)* and the park *(left)* that stood across the street from it. Hillhouse, New Haven's main high school until recent years, stood on Tower Parkway for many years until it was razed in the late fifties, to be replaced by two new Yale residential colleges.

[ 122 ]

DURING THE TWENTIES, there were two legitimate theaters in Hartford. The Shubert chain had taken over the Parson's on American Row, and on February 21, 1921, when this photograph was taken, the show was *Aphrodite*. It had come with a company of three hundred and eight scenes from four weeks in Boston. The Parson's was also a try-out theater, and its last premiere was in 1933, when *Petrified Forest* by Maxwell Anderson, starring Leslie Howard and Humphrey Bogart, opened there. The old Robert's Opera House on Main Street which had been the major house in the late 1800s, was torn down four years earlier. The photograph showing its two horseshoe balconies was taken in 1929 just before the start of demolition. (HC)

THE AMOS BULL HOUSE, seen here in 1922, served as the home of John C. McManus, dealer in stoves and furnaces on the site from 1887 to 1937. The house was originally built in 1788 by Amos Bull, brother of Capt. Aaron Bull. It is now the home of the Connecticut Historical Commission. (HC)

[ 124 ]

GERALD CHAPMAN, center, confers with his counsel during his trial in Hartford for a $2,400,000 mail robbery and the murder of a New Britain policeman in 1924. Connecticut's most notorious criminal of the twenties was convicted and executed in the old Wethersfield State Prison for the policeman's murder. With him are former magistrate Frederick Groehl of New York, Chapman's chief counsel, and Nathan O. Freedman, his junior attorney. (HC)

PRES. CALVIN COOLIDGE has to break his silence to say a few words on Connecticut's first radio station, owned by *The Hartford Courant*, in 1922. With the president is *Courant* publisher Charles Hopkins Clark.

A MAIL TRUCK met the first airmail flight from New York to Hartford in October 1922.

THE FIRST WOMAN PILOT in Connecticut was Mary Goodrich who learned to fly in 1928 and was issued state aircraft license number 3. Miss Goodrich was then a reporter for *The Hartford Courant,* and naturally became its aviation editor. She later married Carl Jenson, who became the *Courant's* real estate editor. (HC)

CONNECTICUT'S "flying governor," John H. Trumbull of Plainville, tried everything, including this glider which he piloted in 1929 during his last term in office. He took up flying at the age of fifty-three after a short flight to Atlantic City. He soloed after his first flying lesson, and cracked up three times while learning to fly. After one bad landing, he took up another plane to "steady his nerves." He died in 1961 at the age of eighty-eight. (HC)

THIS "CARBURETORLESS" PLANE, with its "Wasp" motor built by Pratt & Whitney Aircraft, was tested in Hartford in 1930. It contained a "new device which delivers fuel so accurately to the cylinders that a carburetor is not necessary," according to a contemporary report. (HC)

[ 126 ]

AIMEE SEMPLE McPHERSON HUTTON and her new husband David Hutton flew into East Hartford's new Rentschler Field on their way to Boston in 1931. The field was part of Pratt & Whitney Aircraft, then headed by Frederick B. Rentschler, who moved it from Hartford to East Hartford in 1930. Its new plant then had 400,000 square feet and 30 test houses. (HC)

THE LAST TWO seventeenth-century buildings in Hartford stood at the corner of Main Street and Charter Oak Avenue until 1914, when they were demolished. (HC)

[ 114 ]

PARK STREET near the intersection of Main Street in downtown Hartford looked almost like a country town in the summer of 1916.

FEEDING THE GULLS at Ocean Beach Park in New London was a formal pastime around 1910. Ocean Beach later became the site of a city-owned beach and amusement park.

THESE VIEWS of Chalkers Beach in Old Saybrook and Middle Beach Avenue in Madison show what Connecticut's shorelines looked like in the years between 1910 and 1920.

[ 113 ]

HARTFORD'S MAIN STREET was lit up by streetlights, headlights, and electric signs in this bird's-eye view of the city taken in 1926. The lighted face of the Old State House clock is to the left.

HAYING WAS STILL DONE with horse and wagon in some parts of Connecticut in 1931. Here the late summer crop of meadow grass for winter bedding is gathered in the Guildford salt marshes. (HC)

TOBACCO GROWING has been one of the biggest agricultural industries in Connecticut from colonial days to the present. Drying sheds like this one, photographed in the thirties, used to be extremely common in the Connecticut River Valley, but many have now been torn down as tobacco lands have been taken over for suburban housing tracts. (HC)

THE LEGENDARY *HINDENBURG* hovers over the tower of the Travelers Insurance Companies in 1936.

THE LEADING LITERARY FIGURE in Connecticut from the twenties to the mid-fifties was poet Wallace Stevens, who composed his celebrated poetry on trains, at his home in West Hartford, or during the long walk to his office at the Hartford Accident and Indemnity Company where he was a vice president. In "Of Hartford in a Purple Light," he wrote: "When male light fell on the naked back of town, the river, the railroad were clear, Now every muscle slops away." Stevens died in 1955 at the age of seventy-five after a dual career in insurance and poetry. (HC-Sylvia Salmi)

POETESS Lydia Huntely Sigourney, known in her day as "The Sweet Singer of Hartford," lived and wrote her popular poetry in this mansion built by her merchant husband Charles in 1820. The mansion was demolished in 1938, two years after this photograph was taken. It stood at the foot of Asylum Hill, and was originally surrounded by gardens. These had vanished even in the time of Mrs. Signourney. In a volume published after her death in 1865 she lamented: "The iron horse has since tramped over these premises, annihilated the grove, with its love-consecrated cloister, demolished the rich eastern garden, and with his fiery breath consumed a pair of ancient elms that once guarded its entrance, full of vitality and glory." (HC)

"LITTLE BOY BLUE," Albert (Albie) Booth, probably the most legendary player in the history of Yale football, is shown here in 1931 when he captained the Yale team. Booth grew up in New Haven, went to Hillhouse High, and then spent a year at Milford Prep before he went on to become, during his years at Yale, one of the most sensational broken-field runners the Ivy League has ever seen. He died at age fifty-one in 1959. (HC-AP)

ONE OF THE MOST INTERESTING political figures in Connecticut during the twentieth century was Jasper McLevy, twelve-term Socialist mayor of Bridgeport. First elected in 1933, three years before the photograph was taken, he remained mayor of the city until 1957. He also ran for everything from U.S. senator to governor, polling 138,000 votes for that office in 1938. He was described as an old-time orator, "with eyes like steel and a deep voice which thundered such epithets as 'rankest,' 'disgrace' and 'dishonest' without fear at Democrats and Republicans alike." A right-wing Socialist, he reduced Bridgeport's indebtedness and was celebrated for his parsimony. In refusing to spend money for snow removal, he once said: "God put it there. He'll take it away." (HC)

FORMER GOV. JOHN H. TRUMBULL and Connecticut's top poilitcal boss, Republican Chairman J. Henry Roraback, conferred in 1932, after Trumbull had lost the governorship, and Roraback's political muscle had lost some of its punch. From 1920 until his suicide in 1937, Roraback was a national figure in the Republican party. He was one of the last to abandon a "Draft Coolidge" movement in 1928, and was one of the most effective supporters of the Landon nomination in 1936. But the Depression and the Roosevelt years loosened his grip on power in Connecticut, which had been consistently Republican throughout the twenties.

IGOR SIKORSKY, inventor of the helicopter and founder of Sikorsky Aircraft in Stratford, piloted this first flight of the Vought-Sikorsky VS-300 in 1939. (HC)

A HURRICANE crashing into southern New England on September 21, 1938, toppled and uprooted huge trees. The hurricane caused an estimated $100 million worth of damage, much of it in the coastal areas, and took eighty-five lives.

CONNECTICUT'S FIRST WOMAN GOVERNOR, Ella T. Grasso, graduated from Mount Holyoke College in 1940. The daughter of Italian immigrants, Mrs. Grasso grew up in modest circumstances in Windsor Locks, but attended the private Chaffee School in Windsor before going to Mount Holyoke for her undergraduate and masters work in economics. She served in the state House of Representatives, as Secretary of the State in Connecticut, and in Congress before her election as governor in 1974. (HC)

EDWARD, DUKE OF WINDSOR, paid his first visit to an American manufacturing plant on October 24, 1941, to inspect war material being shipped to Great Britain from the United Aircraft Corporation. With him in this photograph is H. Mansfield Horner, a top UAC executive. The duke signed the company register "Edward." (HC)

WHISTLE-STOP CAMPAIGNS were still the accepted way of getting elected in 1944, when Pres. Franklin D. Roosevelt campaigned for his fourth term. He addressed Hartford people from the back of his railroad car in Union Station on November 4, 1944. (HC)

STAFF SGT. HOMER L. WISE, who lived in Stamford after he completed his army career, won the Congressional Medal of Honor in 1944 for heroism in Magliano, Italy, during World War II. After risking his life to carry a wounded man to medical aid, Sergeant Wise killed three German soldiers with a submachine gun, allowing his platoon to advance; and then, moving ahead of his men, neutralized an enemy machine gun with his fire. Under intense flanking fire, he restored a jammed machine gun on a tank turret and used it so effectively that his battalion was able to secure its objective. He also received the Silver Star, Bronze Star, and three Purple Hearts. During the fifties, he served as an honor guard at the Tomb of the Unknown soldier. He died suddenly in 1974.

SEVEN MARINES from Connecticut who fought in the bitter battle for Iwo Jima posed beneath an anti-aircraft gun on a Coast Guard invasion transport after the battle was won. They were from left to right, Pfc. Sam Barone of Thomsonville, Pfc. Bob Peltier of Unionville, Cpl. Al Bartolucci of Plainville, Cpl. Domenic Serlise of Waterbury, Sgt. Gene Nawrocki of Unionville, Pvt. Anthony Bielik, Jr., of Torrington, and Cpl. John Hutvagner of Bridgeport. The photograph was taken in May of 1945. (HC)

THE USS *Guardfish,* christened in January 1942, was one of the seventy-five submarines built at the Groton shipyard of Electric Boat during World War II. It became one of the navy's distinguished subs during the war and received two presidential unit citations. But in 1961, it was sunk by the navy. (HC-AP)

THIS TEARFUL GOODBYE in the rain was captured in September 1950, when a young soldier left from Hartford's Union Station to serve in the Korean conflict. Harry Batz of *The Hartford Courant* was the photographer. (HC)

AN EIGHTY-THREE-YEAR-OLD MAN overloaded a string of Christmas tree lights with colored bulbs causing the Christmas Eve fire of 1945, which flashed through a Niles Street convalescent home, leaving twenty-one dead. The fire was one of the worst in Connecticut history and led to a law regulating trees in public places. (HC)

WALT KELLY, creator of "Pogo," pictured himself like this in the fifties when his strip was at the height of its popularity. Kelly was raised in Bridgeport and worked for newspapers there before going to the Walt Disney Studios in 1935, where he worked on *Snow White, Dumbo,* and *Fantasia*. He first drew Pogo the Possum in a comic book feature called *Bumbazine and Albert the Alligator* in 1943, but the strip wasn't syndicated until 1949. Kelly died in 1973. This self-caricature is owned by the Museum of Cartoon Art in Greenwich.

OLD NO. 1388, the last of the New Haven Railroad's fleet of steam engines, made her final run in May 1952. She was then sold for scrap. (IIC)

THE MOST WIDESPREAD DISASTER in Connecticut history hit on August 19, 1955, when a dying hurricane named Diane deluged the state with torrential rains that flooded its rivers and streams. When it was all over there were one hundred dead, two hundred seriously injured, and $200 million in damage to the cities and towns of the state. An aerial view at the height of the flooding of Putnam *(left)* shows the force and the fury of the raging flood waters as they coursed through the center of town.

A LIGHTER MOMENT came during the rescue of a cow from the Farmington River in Farmington. The animal was lassoed while churning down the river, and pushed and hauled to safety by volunteer cowboys.

WINSTED'S Mad and Still rivers overflowed their banks and turned the city's main street into a surging waterway that tore away buildings and left rocks and debris in its wake. The northwest Connecticut town was among the hardest hit in the flooding.

FLOOD WATERS tear up a street in Putnam, causing heavy damage to the northeast Connecticut city. The lower photograph shows the same street two weeks later as repair work is carried on. (AP)

FIVE DAYS after the floods, the city of Waterbury still looked like this in some places. The raging Naugatuck River had toppled buildings and carried rubble and silt throughout the low-lying areas of the town.

THE CENTER of Torrington resembled a war zone in the aftermath of the 1955 floods.

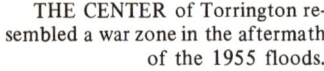

THE FORCE OF THE FLOOD WATERS sheared in half this dry-cleaning business in Naugatuck. The back of the store was made into a disaster area by the swollen Naugatuck River, but the front end was little disturbed, as the clothes hanging neatly at left testify. (AP)

ABRAHAM A. RIBICOFF, the first Jew to serve as governor of Connecticut, took the oath of office from State Supreme Court Justice Raymond E. Baldwin in January 1955. Ribicoff, who grew up in New Britain, had served as a congressman from Connecticut's first district before becoming governor. An early supporter of John F. Kennedy for president, Ribicoff left the governor's office in his second term to serve as secretary of health, education and welfare, and later became a three-term U.S. senator. Judge Baldwin also served as governor and U.S. senator before becoming chief justice. (HC)

JOHN MORAN BAILEY had already been Democratic state chairman for eight years when he celebrated his fiftieth birthday in November 1954, and received this four-footed birthday card halfway through the party at his Hartford home. He remained chairman of his party for thirty years—up to his death in April 1975, and was instrumental in the election of the state's first Jewish governor, Abraham Ribicoff, now U.S. senator, in 1954; and the state's first woman governor, Ella T. Grasso, twenty years later. Bailey was also an early supporter of the presidential candidacy of John F. Kennedy and served as national Democratic chairman under both Kennedy and Lyndon B. Johnson—from 1961 to 1968. With Bailey in the 1954 photograph were his wife and his son John. (HC)

PRES. HARRY S. TRUMAN *(below)* visited Hartford during his presidential campaign in November 1948, and rode through town with some of Connecticut's Democratic candidates. In the foreground is Sen. Brien McMahon of Norwalk who served as senator from 1945 until his death in 1952. Between Truman and McMahon is Abraham Ribicoff, then running for his first term in Congress. Beside Ribicoff in the back seat is Chester Bowles, who was to be elected governor, and who later served as ambassador to India. (HC)

GEN. DWIGHT D. EISENHOWER flashed this victory sign when he visited Hartford on October 22, 1952, during the campaign for his first term as president. In the background is the tower of the Travelers Insurance Companies. (HC)

GOV. JOHN N. DEMPSEY, who served from 1961 to 1971, was the first recent immigrant to serve as Connecticut's chief executive. He returned to his native Ireland in 1970 during his last term as governor and is shown here greeting millworkers in Cahir, the town where he was born. (HC-AP)

POLICE-STUDENT CONFRONTATIONS happened nearly every spring, and in other seasons as well, during the "Silent Fifties" at Yale University. This scene, which shows nightstick-wielding New Haven police chasing students into Yale's Calhoun College, attracted national publicity in 1958 because of the Nazi flag. It was intended to call attention to "Gestapo tactics" of the police, but was misinterpreted. More than fifteen students were arrested in the St. Patrick's Day fracas, and some claimed that police beat them indiscriminately. "Heavier" confrontations were to come in the sixties. (HC-AP)

LOEW'S POLI on Main Street in Hartford was the grandest of the old downtown theaters, all of which were demolished in the sixties for redevelopment projects. Loew's Poli had been an old vaudeville and stock company house as well, but its marble staircases and fancy plaster work were among the first to go, ending an era of wonder in movie-going. New Haven also lost most of its grand old downtown theaters. (HC)

ONE OF HOLLYWOOD'S finest and most enduring actresses was born in Hartford on November 8, 1909. At the age of twelve, Katharine Hepburn was already performing in front of the barn behind her house on Hawthorn Street. She is thought to have acquired her odd accent (uncharacteristic of Hartford, certainly) at Bryn Mawr from which she was graduated in 1928; her yearbook picture shows her with her hair pulled back. She appeared frequently on Connecticut stages since beginning her acting career in the late twenties—at New Haven's legendary Shubert Theatre, at Hartford's Bushnell Memorial, and at the American Shakespeare Theatre in Stratford, where she dressed as a sailor to play Viola in *Twelfth Night* in 1960. And she summers in Fenwick, a borough of Old Saybrook. (HC)

PRES. JOHN F. KENNEDY was congratulated by former Yale president, A. Whitney Griswold, after being awarded an honorary doctor of laws degree from Yale in June 1962. In remarks preceding his commencement address, Kennedy offered to "smoke the clay pipe of friendship with his brother Elis," and acknowledged that now he had "the best of two worlds—a Harvard education and a Yale degree." (HC)

# Index

Adams, Pres. John, 33
Aetna Insurance Company, 35, 54
Allen, Ethan, 24
Alsop and Savage, 34
*American Mercury,* 29
Ames Company, 34
Andros, Maj. Edmund, 20, 42
Ansonia, 34
Archer-Gilligan, Mrs. Amy, 115
Arnold, Capt. Benedict, 24, 26-28
Bailey, John M., 121, 139
Bald, Eddie, 106
Baldwin, Raymond E., 121, 139
Baldwin, Simeon E., 116
Barnum, P. T., 39, 53, 80
Barone, Pfc. Sam, 133
Bartolucci, Cpl. Al, 133
Barton, Doris, 7
Batterson, James Goodwin, 58
Batz, Harry, 134
Beegan, John F., 7
Bielik, Pvt. Anthony, Jr., 133
Bill, George F., 71
Bill, Henry, 43
Bishop, W. F., 104
Block, Adriaen, 12
Block Island, 14
Bogart, Humphrey, 123
Bonaparte, Jerome, 23
Booth, Albert, 130
Booth, Edwin, 54
Booth, John Wilkes, 54
Bowen, Daniel, 21
Bowers, Frederick V., 108
Branford Center, 33
Bridgeport, 39, 50, 53, 55, 63, 66, 69, 75, 76, 77, 79, 80, 81, 88, 90, 99, 103, 104, 108, 116, 118, 121, 130, 133, 135
Bridgeport Public Library, 7
Bristol, 32, 98
Brookfield, 23
Brooklyn, 33
Brown, John, 34
Brown, Thomson and Company, 83, 89
Browning, John M., 55
Bubser's, 59
Bulkeley, Morgan G., 54
Bull, Amos, 124
Bull, Capt. Aaron, 124
Calhoun, John C., 31
Cambridge, 14
Candan, 22
Canterbury, 33
Carr, George F., 99
Carr, George F., Jr., 99

Carrington, Colonel, 27
Case, Lockwood and Brainard, 59
Chaffee and Shaw, 67
Chapin and Burr, 67
Chapman, Gerald, 124
Chappel, Alonzo, 26
Cinque, 34
Clark, Charles Hopkins, 124
Clay, James, 24
Cody, Col. W. F. (Buffalo Bill), 77, 84, 88
Cogswell, Alice, 35
Cogswell, Dr. Mason F., 35
Collins Company, 34
Collinsville, 34
Colt, Samuel, 44, 53
Colt's Armory, 52
Colt's Patent Firearms Manufacturing Company, 32, 34, 44-55
*Connecticut Courant,* 22, 29, 35
*Connecticut Gazette,* 22
Connecticut Historical Society, 7
Connecticut Society of Colonial Dames. 8
Connecticut State Library, 7
Connecticut Tercentenary, 7
Connecticut Writers Project, 7
Cooke, Charles W., 111
Coolidge, Pres. Calvin, 124
Cooper, James Fennimore, 14
Crandall, Prudence, 33
Cross, Wilbur L., 121
Daggett, Napthali, 28
Danbury, 23, 26, 28, 32
Danielson, 102
Davenport, Rev. John, 19-20
Davis, Jefferson, 76
Dempsey, Gov. John N., 140
Devaney, James J., 7
Dexter Plant, C. H.,84
Dickens, Charles, 76
Doolittle, Frances Cooper, 7
Dorchester, 12
East Haddam, 109
East Rock, 30, 34
Eaton, Theophilus, 10, 19, 22
Edward, Duke of Windsor, 132
Eisenhower, Gen. Dwight D., 140
Ellsworth, Oliver, 29
Elm City Flouring Mill, 43
Endicott, John, 16
Enfield, 34
Essex, 29
Eyer, Lieutenant-Colonel, 27
Fairfield, 16
Fairhaven, 30

Falls Village, 34
Farmington, 22, 36, 136
Fenwick, Col. George, 19
Fitch, John, 30
Foch, Marshal Ferdinand, 120
Fort Hill, 16
Fox, G. and Company, 83
Freedman, Nathan O., 124
Gallaudet, Thomas H., 35
Gardiner, David, 19
Gardiner, Lt. Lion, 16, 19
Garrison, William Lloyd, 33
Gilbert, William R., 32
Gillette, William, 109
Glastonbury, 7, 28
Goffe, William, 20
Goodrich, Mary, 125
Goodwin, L. H., 70
Goshen, 28
Gould, Judge James, 31
Grant, Pres. Ulysses S., 58
Grasso, Gov. Ella T., 132, 139
Greenwich, 9
Griswold, A. Whitney, 142
Griswold, Rep. Roger, 33
Groehl, Frederick, 124
Groton, 27, 29, 119, 134
Guilford, 18, 19, 24, 28, 128
Hale, Nathan, 24, 28
Hamden, 7, 30, 34
Hamlin, Hannibal, 48
Hammer, A. M., 97
Harriman, Frank H., 108
Hartford, 9, 10, 13-20, 22, 23, 28-32, 34-37, 39-42, 44, 48, 49, 51-60, 63, 64, 67-76, 79, 82-85, 87-90, 92, 104-107, 109-112, 114-116, 118-121, 123-127, 129, 132, 134, 139-141
*Hartford Courant,* 7, 110, 123, 125, 134
*Hartford Evening Press,* 47
Hartford Fire Insurance Company, 32, 35
*Hartford Times,* 47
Hartnett, Walter J., 116
Hayden, Harry R., 73
Hefflfinger, Pudge, 65
Hennig, Otto, 92
Hepburn, Katharine, 141
Herrick and Cowell, 79
Hoadley, David, 96
Holmes, Capt. William, 12
Holcomb, Marcus H., 116
Holland, John P., 91
Honiss Oyster House, 59
Honiss, T. A., 71
Hooker, Rev. Thomas, 14, 15, 17

[ 143 ]

Hotchkiss and Sons, 43
Howard, Leslie, 123
Hutton, Aimee Semple McPherson, 126
Hutton, David, 126
Hutvagner, Cpl. John, 133
Imlay, William, 30
Jackson, Dr. and Mrs., 60
Jenson, Carl, 125
Johnson, Betty Jean Carper, 7
Johnson, Ernest W., 7
Johnson, Marjorie Leishman, 7
Johnson, Pres. Andrew, 47
Johnson, Pres. Lyndon B., 139
Johnson, Richard, 7
Johnson, Roderick C., 7
Johnson, William Samuel, 29
Jones, Emeline Roberts, 46
Kellogg, J. G., 37
Kelly, Walt, 135
Kennedy, John F., 139, 142
Kimball, P. P., 87
King, Philip, 14, 16-17
Knowlton, Col. Thomas, 28
Korder, Walter R., 13
Lafayette, Marquis de, 76
Lake, Gov. Everett J., 120
Ledyard, Col. William, 27-28
Liefeld, Jean Gamsby, 7
Lincoln, Pres. Abraham, 47, 48, 54, 92
Lind, Jenny, 39
Litchfield, 31
Loew's Poli, 141
Luciano, Michael, 90
Ludlow, Roger, 17
Lyon, Rep. Matthew, 33
Lyons, James, 95
Lyons, Thomas, 94
McLevy, Jasper, 130
McManus, John C., 12
Madison, 113
Manchester, 109
Mansfield, 22, 28, 81
Marcantonio, Mary, 109
Marcantonio, Nicola, 90, 109
Marcantonio, Rosa, 109
Marlin Rockwell, 55, 84
Mason, Capt. John, 16
Massaro, John, 7
Mather, Cotton, 10
Mattabesick, 18
Maxim, Hiram Percy, 106
May, Rev. Samuel, 33
Meigs, Col. Return Jonathan, 28
Meriden, 32
Meriden Brittania Metal Company, 32
Miantinomo, 16
Middletown, 22, 28, 29, 30, 34, 67, 100, 104
Milford, 7, 19, 32
Miller's Casino, 97
Montignani, 77
Montowese, 19
Moody (evangelist), 64
Morgan's Exchange Coffee House, 35
Morse, Samuel F. B., 35
Moseley's New Haven House, 96
Mount Hope, 17
Mystic, 16, 17, 30, 38, 63
Naugatuck, 34, 138
Nawrocki, Sgt. Gene, 133
New Britain, 47, 93, 139
New Haven, 9, 11, 18-22, 24, 28-30, 32, 34, 36, 42, 43, 46, 50, 53-55, 61, 65, 66, 77, 79, 84, 86, 90, 91, 96, 103, 106, 115, 120, 122,

130, 140-142
New Haven Clock Company, 32
New Haven Redevelopment Agency, 7
New London, 18, 22, 27, 28, 30, 40, 78, 113
*New London Summary*, 22
New Town, 14
Newell, Charles R., 67, 104
Newell, Francis, 7
Newell, Isaac, 67
Newell, Walter, 67
North Haven, 7
North, Simon, 30
Norton, Prof. William A., 65
Norwich, 9, 22, 29, 43, 78, 98
Oakley, Annie, 84
Oldham, John, 12, 14
Palmquist, David N., 7
Parker, Col. John H. "Machine Gun," 117
Parson's, 123
Peltier, Pfc. Bob, 122
Pendleton, E., 43
Pettipaug Point, 29
Plainville, 125, 133
Plymouth, 32, 34
Poli's Globe Theater, 108
Pomfret, 24
Pope, Col. A. A., 55, 112
Portland, 30
Pratt and Whitney Company, 84, 119, 126
Putnam, 101, 102, 136, 137
Putnam, Col. Israel, 24, 26, 101
Pyquag, 12
Quinnipliac, 19
Reeve, Judge Tapping, 31
Remington, 55
Rentschler, Frederick B., 126
Ribicoff, Gov. Abraham, 121, 139
Richardson, Henry Hobson, 83
Riggs, Dr. John M., 39
Ripley's Coffee House, 23
Roberts' Opera House, 69, 123
Rogers Brothers, 32
Roosevelt, Pres. Franklin D., 132
Roosevelt, Pres. Theodore, 77
Roraback, J. Henry, 121, 130
Sage, Allen and Company, 83
Salisbury, 28, 34
Sanford and Wadsworth, 30, 32
Sankey (evangelist), 64
Sassacus, 14, 16
Saybrook, 16, 18, 20, 21, 67, 113
Serlise, Col. Domenic, 133
Setzer's Market, 76
Sharp's Rifles, 34, 56-57
Sherman, Roger, 29
Sigourney, Charles, 129
Sigourney, Lydia Huntley, 129
Sikorsky, Igor, 131
Silliman, Benjamin, 65
Smith and Wesson, 32
Smith, E. B., 67
South Glastonbury, 14, 108
South Norwalk, 62
Southport, 62
South Windsor, 30
Squatrito, Marcantonio, 7
Stagg, Amos Alonzo, 65
Stevens, Wallace, 129
Stiles, Ezra, 21
Stone, Captain, 14
Stonington, 9, 18, 22, 29-30
Storrs, 11, 86
Stowe, Harriet Beecher, 109

Stratford, 22, 28, 131, 141
Stratton, Charles S. (Gen. Tom Thumb), 80
Suckiaug, 14
Swan, James, 71
Taft, William Howard. 96, 115
Terry, Eli, 32, 34
Terry, Samuel, 34
Thomas, Seth, 32
Thompson, 99
Thomsonville, 133
Tiffany, Comfort, 102
Torrington, 34, 133, 138
Towne, Charles L., 7
Towne, Ithiel, 66, 96
Travelers Insurance Companies, 58, 140
Treat, Gov. Robert, 20
Trinity College, 51, 54
Trumbull, Gov. John H., 125, 130
Trumbull, Gov. Jonathan, 22
Twain, Mark, 53, 60, 109
Tucker, Sophie, 109
Uncas, 14, 16, 78
Underhill, Capt. John, 16
Unionville, 133
University of Connecticut, 86
Upjohn, Richard Marshall, 54
Van Dusen, Alfred E., 7
Wadsworth, Captain, 20
Warren, A. W. "Lonnie," 73
Warren, Lavinia, 80
Washington, Gen. George, 26
Waterbury, 34, 74, 100, 133, 138
Watertown, 12
Webster, Noah, 31
*Weekly Farmer*, 50
Welch, E. N., 32
Welles, Gideon, 47
Wells, Dr. Horace, 39
West Haven, 97
West Rock, 20
Wethersfield, 12, 15-17
Whalley, Edward, 20
Whipple, Chandler, 7
White, Elmer E., 72
Whitney, Eli, 30, 34, 35
Williams, Roger, 14
Winchester Company, 32, 55, 77
Windham, 28
Windslow, Edward, 12
Windsor, 11, 12, 15-17, 132
Windsor, Locks, 84, 119, 132
Winsted, 32, 136
Winthrop, Fitz-John, 21
Winthrop. John, Jr., 19-20
Wise, Homer L., 133
Woodbury, 22
Wright Brothers, 80
Wyllys, Samuel, 42
Yale, Elihu, 22
Yale University, 9, 19, 21-22, 28, 46, 50, 61, 65, 86, 122
Young, Florence, 7
Ziegfeld, Florenz, 109

[ 144 ]